IN YOUR WRITE MIND

Creative and therapeutic writing exercises to help you feel happier and know yourself better

WENDY STORER

Copyright © 2017 Wendy Storer

First Edition

Published in 2017

ISBN: 9781520406091

CONTENTS

DEAR READER, ... 7

INTRODUCTION 9

USING THIS BOOK 13

ALPHA RELAXATION 15

1: BEING HAPPY 17

EXERCISE 1 ~ FIVE-A-DAY 20

EXERCISE 2 ~ GRATITUDE AWARDS 23

EXERCISE 3 ~ WHAT IS GREAT ABOUT YOU? 24

EXERCISE 4 ~ AFFIRM YOURSELF 26

EXERCISE 5 ~ FORGIVE YOURSELF IN A LETTER 28

EXERCISE 6 ~ CERTIFICATES 30

EXERCISE 7 ~ LISTS FOR A RAINY DAY 31

2: CREATING THE METAPHOR 33

EXERCISE 8 ~ MAKING SENSE OF EMOTIONS 37

EXERCISE 9 ~ FREE VERSE 40

EXERCISE 10 ~ FINDING RELIEF 42

EXERCISE 11 ~ OBJECTIFY A TRAUMA 45

3: WHO ARE YOU?.. 47

EXERCISE 12 ~ GETTING TO KNOW YOU 52

EXERCISE 13 ~ CHARACTER QUESTIONNAIRES 55

EXERCISE 14 ~ WHAT'S IN A WORD? 57

EXERCISE 15 ~ OBJECT POEM 61

EXERCISE 16 ~ A DAY IN THE LIFE OF... 63

EXERCISE 17 ~ INTERIOR MONOLOGUES................... 66

EXERCISE 18 ~ DIALOGUE 68

EXERCISE 19 ~ SETTING AND CHARACTER 71

4: DIARIES AND JOURNALS 75

EXERCISE 20 ~ SPLURGE JOURNAL! 78

EXERCISE 21 ~ REFLECTION JOURNAL........................ 79

EXERCISE 22 ~ DREAM DIARY 80

5: BELIEF MATTERS.. 81

EXERCISE 23 ~ NOTICE WHAT YOU SAY 87

EXERCISE 24 ~ BACK TO YOUR ROOTS 88

EXERCISE 25 –HOW BELIEFS AFFECT YOU 90

EXERCISE 26 ~ BEING EXPLICIT AND IMPLICIT 92

EXERCISE 27 ~ PERSONIFY YOUR BELIEF 94

EXERCISE 28 ~ CHALLENGE YOUR BELIEF 96

EXERCISE 29 ~ OBJECTIFYING A BELIEF 97

EXERCISE 30 ~ INSTALLING NEW BELIEFS 98

6: PROBLEM SOLVING 101

EXERCISE 31 ~ BLOOD LETTING! 103

EXERCISE 32 ~ THE NEGATIVE QUESTIONS 105

EXERCISE 33 ~ WHEN YOU FEEL STUCK 107

EXERCISE 34 ~ YOUR INNER SAGE 109

EXERCISE 35 ~ A STORY OF CONFLICT 110

EXERCISE 36 ~ SLOW DOWN 113

7: PERSPECTIVE 117

EXERCISE 37 ~ WALK A MILE IN THEIR SHOES 119

EXERCISE 38 ~ APPRECIATE YOURSELF 121

EXERCISE 39 ~ PERSPECTIVE OF DISTANCE 123

EXERCISE 40 ~ THE OPTIMIST WITHIN 125

8: GOALS 127

EXERCISE 41 ~ CONTRAST AND CLARITY 129

EXERCISE 42 ~ WHAT YOUR GOALS MEAN 131

EXERCISE 43 ~ SMALL CHUNK YOUR GOALS 133

EXERCISE 44 ~ PLANNING THE MOMENT 135

EXERCISE 45 ~ YOUR PERFECT DAY 137

9: CONNECTING **139**

EXERCISE 46 ~ WRITE A FEELING LETTER **141**

EXERCISE 47 ~ WHAT CAN YOU GIVE? **144**

EXERCISE 48 ~ DEVELOPING EMPATHY **146**

10: FICTIONALISING YOUR LIFE **149**

EXERCISE 49 ~ PLOT YOUR OWN STORY **151**

EXERCISE 50 ~ WRITE YOUR OWN FAIRY TALE **155**

EXERCISE 51 ~ WRITE YOUR OWN FABLE **158**

EXERCISE 52 ~ HOW IS IT GOING TO END? **160**

EXERCISE 53 ~ THE LAST SENTENCE **162**

AFTERWORD **165**

ABOUT THE AUTHOR **167**

Dear Reader,

A pen and paper has always been my confidante of choice. As a teenager, writing down my unhappy, anxious or angry thoughts and feelings was something I did instinctively; either in letter form or scribbled on a random piece of paper. Once out, the painful words and unbearable emotions stopped having any power over me; usually instantly, but if not then, always later. When the emotion was spent, I threw it away. Nobody told me to do this; writing was automatic and has always worked as a pressure valve in my life.

As a teacher, both in mainstream and special education, I was fascinated by children's creative writing. It often seemed as if they were inviting me to read between the lines of their stories in order to understand them – and their experiences – better. One little boy (who was living in care at the time) wrote about a litter of puppies abandoned by their mother. It wasn't a happy story; he wasn't a happy boy. And whilst I knew this story mirrored his own life, I also knew he had refused to talk about it. But through the lines of his story, he was at last able to express some of his feelings about this experience, and this fascinated me.

As someone who wrote stories for a hobby, I began to wonder what my own stories said about my life. Was there was some deeper significance to my choice of characters and events? Was this pressure valve working indirectly, allowing me to communicate my deepest fears and unbearable emotions without me even knowing it?

Later, as a hypnotherapist, I often used to ask my clients to write. We played with their words and tried to reframe situations to lessen their unwelcome emotional impact, and we would often slip into metaphor, both consciously and unconsciously, to explain a situation or a feeling.

Finally, I took a course in Creative Writing Therapy, to better understand the therapeutic role that writing can play in people's lives.

This book is a result of my experiences with writing, as a teacher, therapist, and as a writer. Writing has definitely made me a happier person, as well as given me greater self-knowing.

I hope you find these exercises useful too. Use them as a starting point; then change them, develop them, invent new exercises, write a book ... and beat your own path to happiness with the words you let live on the page.

Wendy x

~

"In creativity I saw light. In the imagination I saw the endless possibility of life, the endless truth, the permanent creation of reality..."

Lemn Sissay

In Your Write Mind

Introduction

Writing about your feelings can help you feel happier. (*1) When you put your thoughts on paper you have a chance to make inner feelings and thoughts into something you can touch and see outside of yourself. When you see your thoughts and feelings on paper, you have a chance to understand yourself better, change the things you want to change and replace negative or unhappy thoughts and feelings with positive, more useful ones.

Writing things down can help you:

- Organise and understand your thoughts
- Give a name to your feelings
- Vent your emotions
- Calm down when you are worried or anxious
- Think about what is important to you
- See things from a different perspective
- Change the way you think and feel
- Create new, positive and more useful thoughts and emotions

---

[1] **Keeping a diary makes you happier**. Psychologists say 'Bridget Jones effect' of writing about feelings helps brain regulate emotions. | Ian Sample | The Guardian, 2009
(http://www.theguardian.com/science/2009/feb/15/psychology-usa)

- Help you to know the real you
- Change the way you behave
- Improve your self-esteem
- Feel calmer, clearer and more relaxed
- Be creative
- Be happier
- Be healthy…

… and yes, even that last one is true. Writing can actually make you healthier as well as all the other benefits. Studies have demonstrated a connection between writing and physical health, (*2,*3)

There are different schools of thought as to why writing works to improve physical, psychological and emotional well-being. The catharsis a person might receive from emotional blood-letting is a temporary response only. The cognitive process which involves the reorganisation, reassessment and/or readjustment of thoughts, emotions and memories is clearly a larger factor.

[2] **Emotional and physical health benefits of expressive writing** | Karen A. Baikie, Kay Wilhelm | The Royal College of Psychiatrists, 2005 (http://apt.rcpsych.org/content/11/5/338.full)
[3] **Expressive Writing: Words That Heal** | James Pennebaker and John Evans | Idyll Arbor 2014

But one thing we do know is that objects which are observed behave differently to unobserved objects under the same conditions. The very act of observation elicits different outcomes from objects, (*4) and that applies to people also.

Writing things down acts an internal observer; perhaps written words have more prominence in the brain than spoken words alone because of the time spent mentally lingering over them while you transfer them to the physical? Or possibly just the act of making words concrete, tangible, gives them more weight.

Either way, words are very powerful.

The words you use have emotions attached to them; for example, PUPPY. Does that word make you feel all gooey and soft inside, or does it make you feel anxious, worried, or something else?

What about this word – SCHOOL? How does that make you feel?

And this word – POWER?

Different people attach different emotional meanings to words, and writing things down helps you to identify what they are. Being aware of your emotions allows you to choose to THINK differently, and if you can find another way to think, you can find a way to FEEL better.

---

[4] **Quantum Theory Demonstrated: Observation Affects Reality** | Weizmann Institute of Science | Science Daily, 1998.
(www.sciencedaily.com/releases/1998/02/980227055013.htm)

The beauty of writing is that you can do it at any time and any place to suit you. If you are upset or anxious, writing down your feelings and thoughts can help instantly; it is like having a friend to talk to.

You can change your life for the better and you are not dependent on anyone else when you write.

You can write almost anything at all; from diaries to lists, to letters, poems, stories, novels, character descriptions, memories, films, affirmations and gratitude lists. You can write about real life or fiction, or combine the two. There is nothing to stop you changing your real life experiences on paper and developing your writing into a story or a poem or a play or a film script; there are no limits to what you can do.

Using this book

The exercises in this book are all about you. Some are directed at the real you – the person you are now, your thoughts and feelings. They are designed to help you find a happier thought, be kind to yourself, solve problems, clarify your goals, uncover some hidden beliefs, and know yourself better. Other exercises give you a chance to be creative and fictionalise your life.

No single exercise will tell you everything you need to know about yourself, or change your life overnight, although some exercises should bring instant relief if you need to feel calm. Each exercise will have a different impact on you, depending on the person you are. There will be some exercises you return to time and time again and others you just don't feel anything for. Some exercises are similar, but different at the same time.

I suggest you start with **Exercise 1 ~ FIVE-A-DAY**, but don't then work through from cover to cover; there will be a right time for each exercise, and I encourage you to pick and choose. Trust your instincts and do whatever feels right for you. Equally, adapt the exercises as and when you feel you need to. There is no wrong way to write – only your way.

Be conscious of the shift these exercises make in your life; be aware of your changing feelings. If you decide to keep a journal of your successes then do so, but don't get bogged down doing this. The change is in the process and not in the recording of the process after it's all over. However, don't let a moment of illumination or clarity escape unnoticed because you have done something to be proud of. The more you appreciate your achievements, the more achievements you will have to appreciate.

Alpha Relaxation

As you work through this book there will be times when your mind is busy and really not in the mood to 'work', be creative or learn. To help you get the most from the exercises and from your writing, you may find a few minutes of relaxation beneficial.

Deep relaxation allows brainwaves to slow down to about 8 - 12 cycles per second to what is called Alpha State, (as compared to the normal Beta State of 13 - 25 cycles per second.) This is the optimum learning state for the brain and also a time where you will have increased access to creativity; the mind is clear and makes connections it would not otherwise make. In Alpha state, the brain is relaxed but aware and focused, as opposed to the Beta state which is where we spend most of our waking lives.

Preparing yourself by accessing Alpha relaxation will increase your self-awareness, creativity and insight.

To get into Alpha State

- Find a comfortable place where you will not be disturbed and take three good deep breaths, making sure to breathe out each time.
- You may wish to close your eyes.
- Now, be aware of your body relaxing, focusing on the top of your head and moving down through your face, your neck, shoulders, arms, hands, fingers, chest, abdomen, groin, thighs, knees, lower legs, ankles, feet and toes…

- Allow the tension to drain away from every area of your body.
- Now count back in your head, from 100 down to zero.
- When you are at zero, open your eyes and start writing.

If you do this short relaxation technique, you will have a better experience of releasing, understanding, creation or whatever you are hoping to achieve from writing.

Having said that, you do not have to do it! Sometimes you are just so eager to get on and write, you do not want to delay. Try varying your experiences and learn what works best for you.

There really is no right or wrong way to navigate the exercises in this book. Don't stress – just do whatever comes naturally, have fun and hopefully, relief and illumination will follow.

1: BEING HAPPY

~

"The point of life is happiness."

The Dalai Lama

~

The exercises in this chapter introduce the notion of writing yourself into a happier frame of mind because happiness matters. Put simply:

- Happiness improves performance and productivity, health and relationships.
- Happy people are more likely to try new things and challenge themselves.
- Happy people have stronger immune systems, cope better with stress and live longer.
- Happy people are more generous, more likeable and more sociable.
- And the happier you are, the more your positive emotions are reinforced.

This all means that happiness is not a luxury, but a necessity.

When a group of researchers from the University of California Riverside studied the link between happiness and success, they discovered that happiness is the key to success, rather than the other way around.

With all these consequences of happiness, shouldn't we all be making it our number one daily goal?

Shouldn't everyone 'try to increase the frequency of positive emotions in their lives by doing things that make them feel happy, even temporarily …'? (*5)

---

[5] **The recipe for success: get happy and you will get ahead in life. Feeling good 'is cause, not effect, of achievement'.** | Kate Ravilious | The Guardian, 2005 (http://www.guardian.co.uk/science/2005/dec/19/uknews)

because the more practised we are at finding the better feeling thought, the happier we will be.

Another study in 2006 found that people experienced greater feelings of life satisfaction if they wrote down their positive experiences, with the good effect lasting up to two weeks. (*6) If you write something which activates a happy feeling, you will feel happier; it's that simple.

Writing isn't about hard work; it's about finding a way to feel good and reinforcing that feeling.

---

[6] **The Google Engineer Teaching Happiness in Three Steps** | David G Allan | BBC, 2014
(http://www.bbc.com/future/story/20141110-googles-algorithm-for-happiness)

Exercise 1 ~ Five-a-Day

"If the only prayer you said was thank you, that would be enough."

Meister Eckhart

~

In 2007 I came across a newspaper article about happiness. (*7) The section which grabbed my interest described an experiment which involved 4 groups of volunteers writing a list of things every night.

- **Group A** wrote at least five things for which they were grateful
- **Group B** wrote at least five hassles in their lives
- **Group C** wrote five things they were better at than others
- **Group D** wrote five major events in their lives

Volunteers were monitored for any personal, mental, physical and emotional changes. At the end of the experiment Groups B, C & D exhibited very few, while Group A showed evidence of increased well-being in all areas. They felt better about life, had greater levels of optimism, fewer physical symptoms, were more helpful and considerate of others, and were more likely to achieve their goals.

---

[7] **"Cheer Up. Here's how…"** | Tal Ben-Shahaar | The Guardian, December 29th 2007

I wholeheartedly recommend you do this beautifully simple exercise before you do anything else in this book, because once you start to shift your focus and concentrate on what is good in your life, you feel happier. When you feel grateful, you feel good about yourself. You cannot feel grateful and feel bad at the same time.

- Every day, write down five things for which you are grateful
- Do this for thirty days
- Observe how you feel

If you want to list more than five things, go ahead, but don't feel you have to. This is supposed to be an affirmation of the good in your life, not an exhausting trial or obligation.

If you do this before you go to bed, it also acts as a positive review of your day and should help to settle you for a good night's sleep.

Developing deeper gratitude

Extend the exercise, by giving yourself reasons for your gratitude. This focuses the mind further and intensifies the positive feelings of well-being that gratitude provides.

And what about the future?

The natural inclination with this exercise is to concentrate on the here and now, but you may also want to try projecting your gratitude onto future events. Be thankful for those things which have not happened yet, but which you dearly want to happen

at some point. Write as if you have already received the subject of your gratitude, and elaborate on it as much as you can.

Even if you are a sceptical person by nature, give yourself permission to enter into the realms of fiction and have a go at this, taking the time to notice the good feelings it arouses within you.

Exercise 2 ~ Gratitude Awards

"Appreciation is a wonderful thing: It makes what is excellent in others belong to us as well."

Voltaire

~

There are many ways to express gratitude and this is one way I came across when working with young children. It works because it engages the imagination, whilst being enjoyable and often amusing.

Quite simply, the exercise is about the notion of rewarding others for giving you a moment of joy in your life.

- As you go about your day, or as you recall it, be aware of any person who has given you a good feeling.
- Write it down, as you would for your five a day and identify the feeling.
- Invent an award for them, for example, "The Comedy Award for the Person who made me laugh most goes to …", "The Kindest Person Award goes to …" or even "The Bending over Backwards to be Helpful Award goes to …"
- If you want to give a reason for the award you can.

Being conscious of the good things other people do will leave YOU feeling warm and appreciative.

Exercise 3 ~ What is Great About You?

"You yourself, as much as anybody in the entire universe, deserve your love & affection."

Buddha

~

Whoever you are, whatever you have done, there are always positives. When you notice a lot of negative self-criticism dominating your thoughts, it is a good idea to take a few moments out of your day and dwell on the positive aspects of you.

- Write down all the positive things you do. Be completely thorough and miss nothing out. Include everything from putting your rubbish in the bin to running a marathon for charity. Be kind to yourself here, and acknowledge all the things you do which impact positively on other lives. Do not be surprised if this takes a long time.
- When you have completed the list, draw a line underneath and then write some more. There will be more.

How does that make you feel?

- Follow up by asking your friends and family to tell you something they appreciate about you. This is very powerful and the more people you ask the better. Add their ideas to your own list.
- Refer to this list whenever you are feeling low.

This is a good exercise to remind yourself of your contribution to the world and the lives of others. It is also a good exercise when you are feeling low in self-esteem or you are harbouring feelings of guilt or regret about something you have done or have not done. It's about seeing yourself with a more positive and objective eye.

Exercise 4 ~ Affirm Yourself

"Once you replace negative thoughts with positive ones, you'll start having positive results."

Willie Nelson

~

Affirmations are a quick and easy way to help you think positively and feel better; they give you the opportunity to preserve and enhance self-worth in the face of your shortcomings, and there is evidence to suggest they work for some people. (*8)

But, writing any old affirmation won't necessarily make you feel any better if at some level you don't believe it, and may actually increase negative feelings towards yourself. So when you do write affirmations it's important to be true to yourself and start with something you believe. For example, instead of writing 'I am always happy,' how about 'I am happy at this moment,' or 'I am happy when I am with friends,'?

The act of writing makes these positive feelings concrete and tangible, and thereby reinforces their power and effectiveness. The most effective affirmations are the ones you make up for yourself, which come from the heart.

---

[8] **Do Self-Affirmations Work? A Revisit: Self-affirmations may or may not help change behaviour and self-esteem.** | Ray Williams | Wired for Success, 2013 (http://www.psychologytoday.com/blog/wired-success/201305/do-self-affirmations-work-revisit)

They should:

- have some grain of truth
- be positive
- be in the present
- be specific

It's a good idea to write your affirmations on separate pieces of card or paper, and leave them lying around your home. This way, when you find one, you can repeat it out loud to remind yourself of the positive message.

Exercise 5 ~ Forgive Yourself in a Letter

"Forgiveness is the attribute of the strong."

Mahatma Gandhi

~

Forgiveness is about letting go of blame and resentment and implies a willingness to move on. When you forgive, you do not necessarily forget but research shows that forgiving a wrong may make it easier to forget. Those people who cannot or will not extend forgiving compassion to themselves, risk increased stress and the possibility of serious health problems. Forgiveness, therefore, plays a key role in emotional, mental and physical well-being, and can, in turn, improve the health of family and community. (*9)

One way you can help yourself to feel better about past events and behaviours is to allow the 'past you' and the 'present you' to interact.

There is plenty of research to back this up, for example:
a) **Forgiving a Wrong May Actually Make It Easier to Forget** | Saima Noreen | Association for Psychological Science, 2014 (http://www.psychologicalscience.org/index.php/news/releases/forgiving-a-wrong-may-actually-make-it-easier-to-forget.html)
b) **Forgive yourself if you want to live longer: Those lacking 'self-compassion' get stressed more easily and let it affect them over a longer period of time – leading to serious health problems**. | Adam Withnall | The Independent, 2014 (http://www.independent.co.uk/news/science/forgive-yourself-if-you-want-to-live-longer-scientists-say-9248685.html)
c) **The New Science of Forgiveness** | Everett L. Worthington, Jr. | Greater Good Science Centre | University of California, Berkeley. 2004 (http://greatergood.berkeley.edu/article/item/the_new_science_of_forgiveness)

Writing to yourself is a very powerful way of acknowledging what you have learned in life and how it has helped you to be where you are now.

- Write a letter to your younger self, beginning Dear Me.
- If there is a specific thing you want to forgive, acknowledge this in your letter as much as you feel you need to, and tell 'past you' that you are happy to let this go.
- Also tell 'past you' what you have achieved in your life, what you might expect to happen over the years and tell them how they got through the bad times and how they enjoyed the good times.
- Give 'past you' the benefit of your 'what you know now' knowledge.
- Tell 'past you' you forgive them, and remember to send back some love.

Whatever has happened in your past, the simple fact is that you made it through; you are here today, trying to find ways to feel happier, and better about yourself. The past is gone. You are in the present.

Exercise 6 ~ Certificates

"The more you praise and celebrate your life, the more there is in life to celebrate."

Oprah Winfrey

~

When you were a child, did you get certificates for swimming or for being neat with your writing or winning a fancy dress competition? Can you remember the feeling you had when you were given a sticker for being brave at the dentist? Or maybe you never did get that recognition for something good that you did. Well, it's never too late!

If you did something that you felt proud of and never received recognition for, now's the time to claim it.

- Write yourself a certificate to acknowledge something you feel deserves to be appreciated.
- Write down what the certificate is for and praise yourself for your efforts with gold stars, 10/10, or some great big ticks! Do whatever you need to make you smile, and go ahead, feel good.

You may think that this exercise is aimed at children, but it works just as well with adults. Seriously.

Exercise 7 ~ Lists For a Rainy Day

"A man cannot be comfortable without his own approval."

Mark Twain

~

So, we all have rainy days. I'm talking about the metaphorical rainy day here; those days when you need a bit more love and appreciation and the world outside just doesn't seem to get how awesome you really are. One answer, instead of feeling bad, is to write a list. Lists are quick, usually easy, and fun. They can be about anything at all as long as they bolster your sense of self, are positive, and personal.

Here are some ideas:

- Successful moments in my life
- People who have loved me / people I love
- Things I have overcome and turned to my advantage
- Things which make me feel good
- The best holidays of my life
- The beautiful world around me
- Kind things people have said to me / I have said to others
- Twenty things I could do to make someone else smile

Lists work because what you think affects how you feel, which affects how you act, which in turn affects what you think, which affects how you feel, which affects how you act ...

Writing a feel-good list breaks that cycle long enough for you to allow yourself to think differently, feel better, and act accordingly.

2: CREATING THE METAPHOR

~

"Metaphors have a way of holding the most truth in the least space."

Orson Scott Card

~

Metaphor is from the Greek word metaphora, meaning 'a transfer.' When we reach for metaphors in our writing, we are essentially building a bridge between thought and emotions, avoiding the ego defence mechanisms of resistance and denial, and speaking in code to the subconscious mind. This allows us to alter our perspective, be flexible with our thoughts, put uncomfortable emotions at a distance and see them more objectively, and be creative. Tackling problems with metaphors can provide you with the flashes of relief you need in order to find a solution.

When working as a hypnotherapist, I always found metaphors a really useful tool for:

- Uncovering hidden emotions,
- Challenging emotions and behaviours which were not useful, and
- Creating solutions which might otherwise have been resisted.

By removing the immediate associations and resistances a client had about a specific emotion or situation, they were able to experience and understand it in a less threatening (or better still, a non-threatening) way.

A client of mine comes to mind. For a myriad of reasons, she was entirely consumed with negativity and convinced that she was worthless. It was very difficult to make any progress with her and it was as if she was stuck.

I wanted her to see that whatever had influenced her past, she could move on, and in conversation I used a metaphor of the seasons, pointing out how change is inevitable. I talked about trees losing their leaves and plants apparently sleeping over winter, only to find new growth and sunlight in the spring and summer.

She understood the metaphor but counteracted it immediately, saying that all the trees in her life had been chopped down and would never grow again! So we talked about what happened next; about how fallen trees can provide a home for nature and how some will sprout new leaves and branches, drawing upon stored reserves in the roots. Sometimes trees will not produce sprouts from their roots and will begin to decay, but even then, all the goodness from that tree will sink back into the land to nourish growth of a different kind.

This was the first time I saw a glimmer of hope in my client's eyes. It didn't matter how negative she was being, there was always some room for hope and the possibility of change.

Many of the exercises in this book will draw on metaphor. The key to using metaphors therapeutically is to find ones you are happy with. It's also worth remembering, that it isn't about creating a great work of literature; it's about greater self-awareness.

Don't worry about mixing your metaphors, or making sense to anyone but yourself. Just let yourself go here; let your unconscious mind come out with whatever it needs to, in order to make sense of the way you feel in this situation.

Exercise 8 ~ Making Sense of Emotions

"You don't see something until you have the right metaphor to let you perceive it."

Robert Stetson Shaw

~

The following two-part exercise uses the five senses to create metaphors for emotions. This is something you can return to time and again, adding new metaphors, and essentially creating your own emotion thesaurus.

In the short term, you may find that your words allow you a little distance from an unpleasant emotion, while at the same time help to explain it. In the long term, you may find that you start to think differently, more creatively, and express yourself more easily. It works for positive emotions – joy, excitement, or love for example – as well as the more negative ones you would rather not feel.

This creative approach to emotional expression is also good for writing fiction when you're trying to show not tell.

Part One

- Make a list of all the emotions you have ever felt. (Well, a few at least!)
- Make a list of about twenty different sounds. Try to be specific about who or what makes the sound, just to anchor it in reality. So for example, you would write a baby crying, rather than crying; a church bell ringing, rather than ringing.
- Repeat this process for smells. Again, try to pick out distinctive smells which mean something to you; sweet lavender, rancid fish, freshly baked bread, for example.
- Do the same for notable tastes. Sour apple, bitter lemon, mature cheese.
- Make another list of verbs, of actions, of things people do. (Run, dance, jump etc.)
- Final list – think about textures; think about the way something feels to the touch.

Part Two

- Now, choose one emotion – maybe something which is particularly relevant to you at this point in time – and pick out, from your carefully constructed lists, one sound, smell, taste, action, or texture, which would describe that emotion.
- Use (some or all of) your chosen words to create a sentence.
- Do you feel this adequately expresses the emotion you want to describe?
- Do you need to alter or embellish the metaphor to give your image all the light and shade it needs to come to life?

Have fun with this exercise. Play with different images, and repeat for different emotions.

Exercise 9 ~ Free Verse

"Poetry begins in trivial metaphors, pretty metaphors, grace metaphors, and goes on to the profoundest thinking that we have."

Robert Frost

~

If you've done Exercise 8, you will now have a clearer idea about how a particular emotion sounds, smells, tastes, and so on. Extending this experiment with metaphors puts you in the position of a poet. Poetry allows you to express thoughts, feelings and experiences through metaphor, but adds rhythm and sometimes rhymes to create different shapes. It is a different art to prose, which suits some people better than others. I love this explanation for the difference between poetry and prose from the Poetry Foundation. (*10)

"... Among other things, prose is principally an ethical project, while poetry is amoral, a tampering with truths ... Poetry creates its own truth, which at times is the same truth as the world's, and sometimes not."

Whilst many forms of poetry have rules to do with rhyme scheme and meter, free verse has no such rules; you are free to concentrate on your words,

---

[10] **The Difference Between Poetry and Prose, from a 1973 discussion with Gunnar Harding**. | Martin Earl | Poetry Foundation, 2012 (http://www.poetryfoundation.org/harriet/2012/04/the-difference-between-poetry-and-prose/)

images and metaphors rather than be bound by structure.

For this exercise:

- Choose one emotion which is troubling you.
- Spend a minute or two focusing on that word, then write down anything and everything you associate with it – words, phrases, sensory metaphors, simile, and words which look and sound like the things you want to express.
- Think about how this thing, this emotion, makes you feel, and how it affects others. Write it down.

This is a chance to think freely and just let all ideas flow. You are collecting ideas here, and might not even do this in one session; it's something you can return to later.

- Find a way to organise these ideas; to paint a picture with words.
- Experiment with the order of things, verse length, line breaks, punctuation.
- Use line breaks to create rhythm or to emphasise an idea.

There's no wrong way with free verse, or with the interpretation of your thoughts and feelings into a picture with words. Whatever you do is right for you.

Exercise 10 ~ Finding Relief

"Relief lets the air out of the Tire of Pain."

Adriana Trigiani

~

Once you have created a metaphor for an emotion, you have the chance to adjust your thinking or feeling about that situation. This exercise can help you to think or feel differently, but it is also useful for an uncomfortable situation, an obstacle or problem you can't quite see yourself clear of. The trick here is finding a moment of relief from the problem, and in that relief, you have a chance to find an answer, or at least think differently.

I was working with a young man some years ago whose father had walked out and his mother wasn't coping alone. Not surprisingly, he suffered from feelings of abandonment, low self-esteem, and was very withdrawn. He described his situation as being like 'stuck in a broken-down car in the middle of nowhere with vultures dive-bombing me every five minutes.' His description of the scene was bleak, full of images of death and decay, without anything positive to draw on. Except that he constantly talked about being 'nowhere' and this gave us something to work with.

I asked him to describe the 'edges of nowhere.' Reluctantly he wrote a description of what it might be like, including a garage with mechanics, and shops with nice food. I wanted him to imagine a way to get to the 'edges of nowhere' so he wrote about an eagle he had befriended. He sent this eagle off to the town to get the parts he needed to repair the car himself. The story ended with him driving into town, the eagle flying ahead, and him being offered a job in the garage!

It was the relief he needed from his situation. He went with the process and it had lasting effects. He now works in a local garage and we still say hello.

So now it's your turn.

- Recall a situation which is troubling/has troubled you.
- Create a metaphor for this situation.
- Now find a way to alter, manage, or extract yourself from this situation; be imaginative and do whatever is needed to make it a positive experience with positive associations.

It's important to become part of the metaphorical world and to fully inhabit that place. In doing this, the metaphorical situation then becomes the obstacle you have to overcome – not the real situation.

- Describe your solution. What does relief look like? Sound like? Smell like? Taste like? Feel like? Do you feel warm? Safe? Are you smiling? Do you have food? Has the sun come out? Is the sky blue?

Really take time to describe the positive experience of being free from your problem and you will feel the benefits immediately. It's the relief which is important here.

This exercise will send a powerful message to your unconscious mind that there is a solution. At worst, it will give you a break from your problem. At best, that break is all you need to allow a real life solution to come to you.

Exercise 11 ~ Objectify a Trauma

"Anything I cannot transform into something marvellous, I let go."

Anais Nin

~

This exercise is similar to the previous exercise, except that you are specifically dealing with traumatic events here. As with the previous exercise, creating a metaphor will help disconnect you from the emotional impact of a past trauma, allowing you to revisit a traumatic event without being re-traumatized by the act of remembering. (*11) Acknowledging its presence in your psyche is the first step in reducing or eradicating its affect on you in the present.

By creating an object in your mind as a symbol of your trauma or disease, you have something tangible to work with.

It's helpful to get into Alpha State for this exercise since it relaxes your mind and allows you freedom from thought for a while, which also allows freedom from resistance. When you stop resisting, you allow solutions in. Find a quiet place to sit, uninterrupted for a few minutes.

---

[11] For more on this, take a look at **The Role of Metaphor in Recovery from Trauma** | Susan Lien Whigham | First published at www.theschizophreniamyth.com, 2006
(http://www.cleanlanguage.co.uk/articles/articles/291/1/Role-of-Metaphor-in-Recovery-from-Trauma/Page1.html)

- Take some deep breaths in and release each breath, slowly. With every release, concentrate releasing any tension in your body. When you feel relaxed, close your eyes and count backwards in your head from 100 down to 1.
- Put a picture in your mind, of something which represents the issue you want to deal with. Any picture, any object, anything which resonates with you.
- Imagine its colour, shape, texture, smell and the sound it will make. Whatever image comes to mind is the right one for you.
- Give it a name.

It is important NOT to relive the actual event or connect your emotions to this image. Keep the experience object oriented at all times.

- Make the item as real in your mind as you can.
- Then write down everything that you have created. Get a real sense of this object in your writing and be as descriptive as you can.
- Now, write a story or a poem, or a maybe a letter to the object.
- OR you may choose to personify the object and see life from your object's point of view.

Whatever you choose to do with your object, it is the right thing for you. (There are no wrong outcomes here.) The creative challenge of this exercise is to now find a way to work with this object to your benefit. Or, failing that, eradicate it from your life.

3: WHO ARE YOU?

~

"Self-knowledge is essential not only to writing, but to doing almost anything really well. It allows you to work through from a deep place – from the deep, dark corners of your subconscious mind."

Meg Rosoff

~

There has been much written and studied about the therapeutic benefits of autobiographical writing. I think it's only natural to want to look back on your life and take stock. Every life is unique and every person will have a different understanding of shared or similar experiences. Chances are, we will not have processed the emotional implications and attachments for a large number of those experiences; either we are too busy living, moving on to the next thing, or possibly we don't want to attach the emotions to the experience. Maybe there are some things we would just like to run away from and forget?

But we cannot let an uncomfortable or unpleasant feeling go free from our psyche unless we know what it is.

Our mind is like an iceberg; the tip of the iceberg is our conscious mind, while the huge frozen block hidden from view and supporting everything else is our unconscious mind. If we genuinely want to move on and leave difficult emotions behind, we are going to need some degree of thaw; at least, just enough to release whatever it is that might be holding us back.

When writing an autobiography, you recall experiences and remember the things which have brought you to where you are now. You give yourself the opportunity to express and process your feelings and thoughts, get clear about events and their consequences, and develop your sense of self.

All writing is to some extent autobiographical. When you choose to write about anything, what you bring to it is your understanding of it. Whether you know about something first or second hand, it will still be influenced by you, the writer. Wherever you draw inspiration from – a newspaper article, a painting, a song, letters, the internet, history, books, maps, artefacts, or dreams, for example – creativity will still force you to delve into the depths of your unconscious mind, making links and sparking off new ideas. And that is why analysing your fiction writing can be a great move towards better self-understanding.

You don't have to be writing about your traumas or struggling with problems in your writing but you will inevitably find that the more you write, the more you repeat themes. These themes will most likely have some significance for you, and I would venture to say they are your unconscious mind trying to work through something and make sense of it.

- What themes come up in your writing?
- What do you see repeated time and again?
- What are your preferred genre, style, and tone?
- What phrases or words do you use frequently?
- What does your writing say about your life?

There are no one-size-fits-all meanings to the answers of these questions; for example, if abandonment is a recurring theme in your writing it might suggest you were working through your own fears of abandonment in the past, the future, or that you were once abandoned, or that you were once someone who abandoned another. Or it might have some completely different interpretation! The important thing is to make the connections yourself, and over time, consider your own answers.

Alternatively, you can consciously use yourself as a starting point for fiction. From a purely creative point of view, here you are with a ready-made character and a whole bunch of experiences to draw on, which you are free to exaggerate, alter or wipe out as and how you choose, because in your fictional world you are in total control. Make your character larger than life, create new story lines, change the emphasis or point of view, have fun, take risks, add to the drama …

Your life is your biggest story and you have a starring role as the main character.

In the following exercises you can choose to write openly and honestly about yourself and your experiences, which is both a direct and straightforward way of developing greater self-awareness.

However, if you are not yet ready (or able) to be that candid or look at things close up, you may choose to invent other characters or situations to do it for you. These may well be metaphors for you and your life or they may be total fiction; you don't need to analyse that while you're writing; your unconscious mind will do all the work here.

This is your chance to let go, to use your imagination to work through problematic thoughts, behaviours and feelings, and to create your life exactly how you want it to be.

This is your chance to reinvent yourself.

Exercise 12 ~ Getting to Know You

"Every secret of a writer's soul, every experience of his life, every quality of his mind, is written large in his works."

Virginia Woolf

~

Characters are the whole point of stories. We invest in characters emotionally, and our feelings about them are the hooks which keep us reading. Without characters, there are no stories, so you have to get them right.

In fiction, main characters need to be interesting, vivid, and sometimes larger than life. We don't have to like them, but we do need to care about them, and they must have flaws and problems because no one is perfect (and we won't believe in them if they are.) They need to be dynamic too; static characters that don't grow, adapt, or change are pointless in a story.

You are the main character in your own story, and as that person, it's important to fulfil all these functions. This two-part exercise is a good place to start thinking about who you really are, and what makes you the main character in the story of your life.

Part 1 ~ Write 4 paragraphs about you, outlined below

- How are you interesting? What sets you apart from others? What makes you bigger, funnier, meaner, or stronger than others? In what ways do you excel?

- Why should other people care about you? You're never going to please all of the people all of the time, but think about the reasons why we should care about you. Perhaps you have overcome some difficult obstacles, or have been especially kind to others, or maybe you have some desirable qualities (a special skill, a passion, a sense of humour, and so on).

- What are your flaws and/or problems? Go easy on yourself here. We're talking annoying little habits or strange idiosyncrasies, nothing more. This is an exercise in appreciating what makes you uniquely human.

- And how will you grow? How will you change in the future? We are interested in characters who go on a journey, have conflict in their lives, and grow as a result of overcoming obstacles. How do you relate to that in your life? If you feel stuck, how might you change in the future?

Part 2 ~ Fictionalise

- Take each paragraph and try to disassociate it from yourself. Try to see this person as a character in a story – someone who is not you. What would you do to make this character even more interesting? Or funny? Scary? Ugly? Sad? How would you make this character larger than life? Why should we care about them? How might they overcome their problems? How might they grow over time?

- Write a whole new character description for this person, making them as real as you can, and do your best to give this character a hopeful outlook on life.

What you have done in this exercise is to step outside of yourself and play with the possibilities of who you are and who you might become. You have opened the doors to a more objective view of yourself and the potential for change.

A creative writing therapy client once told me this exercise acted as a kind of blueprint for her future; specifically the question of how she might overcome her problems. She thought it worked because giving advice to someone else is so much easier than giving it to oneself, except that this exercise took her full circle when she realised the fictional character she had created, was really her.

Exercise 13 ~ Character Questionnaires

"It begins with a character, usually, and once he stands up on his feet and begins to move, all I can do is trot along behind him with a paper and pencil trying to keep up long enough to put down what he says and does."

William Faulkner

~

Another way to get to know your (real or fictional) character is to write a questionnaire and fill in the answers. Initially, a questionnaire to yourself may seem pointless and uncreative – you already know all the answers, after all – but that's where the creativity comes in. You need to ask challenging questions and plumb hidden depths. The questions themselves will be revealing, but if you keep digging the answers you give yourself may both surprise and entertain you.

Ask open questions; the ones which you cannot answer with YES or NO, and choose searching questions which will elicit answers which reveal something about you/your character's inner world.

It is worth remembering that the questions people ask, often reveal as much about themselves as they do about the person answering them.

What do your questions say about you?

Here are a few sample questions to start you off …

- What one thing would this character change about their appearance?
- Write something intriguing about this character's family
- What's the worst / best thing anyone ever did to this character?
- What's the worst / best thing this character ever did to anyone else?
- Where does your character go when he's angry?
- What makes your character laugh out loud?
- Who does your character love?
- What is your character ashamed of?
- What is your character proud of?
- What does your character want most in the world?
- What lengths would he/she go to, to get it?
- What stands in his way?
- What one word best describes your character? …

Exercise 14 ~ What's in a Word?

"Words are singularly the most powerful force available to humanity."

Yehuda Berg

~

In everyday conversation, we do not often have the time or luxury of examining the words we are using, and most words will be spoken without a second thought. We know what they mean, and we fit them into sentences and go about our business. And that is quite understandable; if we were to stop and rethink the deeper meanings of each and every word or sentence we uttered, every time we spoke, we would never say anything. But words are very powerful. Sometimes they reveal more about our innermost thoughts than we realise because words have a unique and personal resonance.

When you have a thought, you create an electrical impulse in the brain. This triggers a chemical emotional reaction, which is followed by a physical manifestation. Or to put it another way, a word can create an emotion, which will (on an unconscious level) determine how you behave. Different people attach different meanings to words, and that is why it's important for you to identify the deeper meanings of the words you use and the emotions you attach to them.

By being aware of the emotional connections that words have, you have the power to use them positively and beneficially. Your thoughts decide your feelings. By paying attention to the words you use, you can change your life.

This exercise can help you understand the associations you have with certain words, and find an alternative way to express yourself. Having a more positive emotional resonance with the words you use will create improved feelings in your life.

- Think of a character trait that you have and feel negatively towards. For example, laziness.
- Write this down on paper and disassociate it from yourself. It is a word on paper, nothing to do with you.
- Now create a general list of words (or phrases) which could be associated with this trait. Your own associations are the ones which matter here. For example, slow, idle, relaxed, calm, not stressing out, taking life at your own pace, work-shy...
- Divide the words into two lists – one negative and one positive. Again, your own associations are what matter.
  EG Negative: slow, idle, work-shy...
  Positive: relaxed, calm, not stressing out, taking life at your own pace...

- Now, find one word (or phrase) of positive resonance to replace each negative word and write a new list. You are not looking for the opposite here. You are looking for a word which has a similar meaning, but which has a more positive tone. The object is to end up with a list of words which have wholly positive associations. EG Slow might become measured, idle might become still, work-shy might become independent ...
- Now write a paragraph describing you, using this positive list. If it helps to write in the third person (he, she, him, her instead of I, me) then do so.

By now, you should have an alternative view of yourself and greater insight into the hidden meanings of the words you use.

Follow on: Removing negative associations to an event

You can also do this exercise for a situation which has caused you some grief, upset or feelings you would rather not have.

- Simply write an account of this event, and then underline all the words with negative associations for you.
- Rewrite the account, replacing the negative words with positive ones.
- Read it back to yourself, and allow yourself to feel differently about this event from now on.

This has a surprisingly powerful impact on the way you feel about things. One of my clients wrote about a 'shameful' episode in her life when she had 'embarrassed' herself in front of a family member. She rewrote her account of the incident, replacing the negatively charged words with positive ones, and found a way to laugh at the mishap which led towards forgiveness and ultimately mended the rift between her and her sister.

The secret to altering the word polarity is to find alternatives which are relevant and meaningful to you.

Exercise 15 ~ Object Poem

"The writing of a poem is like a child throwing stones into a mineshaft. You compose first, then you listen for the reverberation."

James Fenton

~

Imagine for a moment that you are not who you are; imagine you are not even a person, but an object. Take a look around and find an object you are drawn to. It doesn't matter what it is; maybe in your home, or work environment? Or maybe you could go outside and find something there?

In this exercise, you are writing from the point of view of that object. The poem will be formed from the answers to a series of questions (below).

When you have chosen an object, answer the following questions:

- What are you? (This is the first line of your poem. EG I am a small shell…)
- What do you look, sound, feel, smell and/or taste like? (Use your senses to describe your new self.)
- How do you feel?
- How do you make others feel?
- What is your fondest dream?
- And your worst nightmare?
- What are you really good at?

- What one thing would you change about your life if you could?
- What one thing would change in the world, if you could?
- What makes you happy?
- If you could be anywhere, where would that be?
- Do you have any words of wisdom to pass on to your descendants?
- How would you like to be remembered?
- Do you have any more questions you would like to answer? If so, what are they?

When you have finished this exercise, look at your answers.

Many people find they have written from the heart – that is, from their own hearts; meaning that these answers are actually about them. Somehow, it is easier to write about ourselves when we disassociate from our internal worlds and project those feelings onto an inanimate object.

Exercise 16 ~ A Day in the Life of...

"You take people, you put them on a journey, you give them peril, you find out who they really are."

Joss Whedon

~

This exercise sends you on a journey of the unexpected. It's a bit like one of the childhood 'what if' games where a friend would ask (for example) what would happen if you saw a tiger in the street? You cannot possibly know, but just thinking about it opens up a whole world of possibilities and forces you to think about yourself in a way you might not usually.

Alternatively, you can use this as a starting point for a fictional journey, putting an imagined character through his/her paces. However, if you are using a fictional character start with a short character description of that person, just so you know a little about who you are dealing with.

Have fun with this and be creative. It's a chance to turn your day into something extraordinary.

- Think of ten 'out of the blue' events which might happen to you/your character in a day. By all means write the mundane, (shopping, cleaning the car, making dinner etc) but use your imagination to create different, unusual, exciting events too.
- Write them all down on separate pieces of paper, and fold them up so you cannot see what is written on each one.
- Start to write your day, in first person, present tense. (For example, I walk into the kitchen and there are five people sat at the table, all staring at me...)
- Pick one folded 'out of the blue' event at random, and incorporate this into your narrative. How will you/your character react? What happens as a result of this?
- Continue writing for a few minutes, and then repeat the last instruction. And again and again... Be creative. Look for imaginative answers.
- Stop when you have exhausted all the possibilities or when you feel this situation has come to a natural end.

To develop this you might like to try:

- Changing the emotions involved, so that for example if you/your character found something scary, maybe you could write it again with them finding the same event thrilling and exciting.
- Creating a new character for you/your first character to interact with; a partner, relative, or stranger.
- You can also use this exercise to plan for an important event as a way of thinking through all the possible scenarios ahead of the time. (See **Exercise 44 ~ Planning the Moment**)

Exercise 17 ~ Interior Monologues

"Everyone who wills can hear the inner voice."

Mahatma Gandhi

~

Our interior monologues provide us with a window to self-awareness. They give us the words which allow us to identify and deal with information about our emotions, thoughts and behaviour, and at an even more basic level, tell us we are alive, unique and of value.

We all have a measure of self-talk going on at all times; we may, or may not pay this monologue conscious attention. If we do listen to it, it's worth listening properly and understanding whether or not this self-talk is valid and useful, or just plain destructive. If we don't listen to it, it's about time we gave it some breathing space, because lurking here in the self-talk are the hidden beliefs which control our thoughts, feelings and behaviours. (More about hidden beliefs later.)

Here is one way to connect to your interior monologue.

- Remember a good day in your life.
- Write a first person, present tense account of that day – as if it is actually happening now.
- Take care to remember how it made/makes you feel.
- Consider how the events of the day were affected by your personality. What made this day special for the kind of person you are?

Follow on

- Use the same experience, and repeat this exercise for a character you have created.
- How different is the character from you?
- How does he/she think and feel?
- Would you and this character like to have a discussion about these events and your different/similar thoughts on the day? If so, perhaps you could write that as a dialogue. (See **Exercise 18** for more on dialogue.)

Seeing this experience from an alternative (objective) point of view can help you to identify your own inner monologue as something different to that of another; something that is unique to you.

Exercise 18 ~ Dialogue

"He who knows others is wise; he who knows himself is enlightened."

Lao Tzu

~

Having conversations with others is a very good way to understand yourself and where you're coming from. Having imaginary conversations works just as well as having real ones, plus you can make the other person say whatever you want them to say, which is also revealing about yourself.

So here are a few dialogue ideas for things which may or may not help you understand yourself better, or which may be useful starting points for further analysis or a work of fiction. Write your dialogue as talking heads – using a 'he said/she said' format – and think about the words and phrases this character might use to express themselves.

- Write a dialogue between two people talking about you. One person only says positive things, the other only negative. How does that make you feel?
- Think of something you feel very strongly about and discuss it with someone who disagrees with you. How does it affect you to hear their point of view?
- Your partner/best friend/mother has read your diary and discovered something about you which you would rather have kept secret. Discuss the revelations with this other person.
- You are upset about something in a public place; a library, bus stop, or café for example. A stranger befriends you and is able to comfort you. What do they say? How do they make you feel better?
- You want to make a good impression. Maybe you are at an interview, on a blind date, or in court, for example. What do you tell another person about yourself to win them over?

Follow on

Behavioural psychologists estimate that only 7% of communication involves actual words; a whopping 55% of communication is done through body language, and the rest is down to the way you say those words – pitch, volume, tone etc. Real people are more than 'talking heads' and their words are never spoken in isolation.

When writing dialogue, a supporting narrative will help to create a more holistic and realistic scene. Behavioural observations are just as important as the words your characters use. Think about the physical movements of the speakers, and what happens in the moments where there is silence. Consider the physical landscape.

- Rewrite your piece of dialogue but this time, add the context. I.E. The actions, thoughts and behaviour of the speakers, as well as details about the environment, or setting.

Exercise 19 ~ Setting and Character

"We are what we see. We are products of our surroundings."

Amber Valletta

~

What does your environment say about you? Are you a neat freak or a hoarder? Do you tidy, but not clean? Do you like everything to be matching, designer labelled, valuable? Or do you prefer second-hand and family heirlooms?

There are endless reasons for the choices you make about your home environment, but being aware of those reasons might also reveal something about your character which you have never brought consciously to the fore. When we look at the home or work environment of another person, even if we aren't consciously trying to glean information about that person, we can't help but learn something about them.

In fiction, setting (place, time, and atmosphere) communicates information about the characters which inhabit it. This exercise can be used as a starting point for fiction as well as to reveal something about your own life.

Part 1

- Describe Character A's main living space (without them in it). Character A might be you – or a fictional character.
- Don't make any value judgements or try to justify anything. Describe the scene as it is, but don't feel you have to describe every single thing. Do your best to convey the order/disorder, décor, furnishings etc, so that others would get a real sense of where everything is and why it's there.
- Remember to use the five senses when you are writing about Setting.

Part 2

- Now imagine Character B (either a stranger to character A or a friend/relative) enters this room.
- What do they see? (Probably not everything.) They will notice different things, depending on the kind of person they are.
- Again, just try to see this scene through Character B's eyes, without judgements at this stage.

Part 3

- Now it's time to set your imagination to work; time to make those judgements!
- How does Character B react?
- What conclusions might he/she reach about Character A?
- What might they think about Character A?
- How might they feel towards him/her?
- What might they do?
- What happens next?

The possibilities for this exercise are endless. If you are writing about your own environment, focusing on the minutiae of what you have collected around you, you might discover something new about yourself.

If you are using this as a starting point for fiction, make sure that there is something in Character A's room which lends itself to ask questions. Leave clues which will force the reader to ask questions. Why are those drawers open and the contents spilling out? Why don't the curtains match? What is that stain on the carpet? Make the setting an exciting and interesting place which reveals character.

4: DIARIES AND JOURNALS

~

"Writing in a journal ... offers a place where you can hold a deliberate, thoughtful conversation with yourself."

Robin S. Sharma

~

There is no doubt that writing a personal diary or journal of your life will bring rewards. Indeed, 'keeping a diary, making up poetry and scribbling down song lyrics can help people get over emotional distress' (*12), but it also offers you the opportunity for clarity, deeper understanding of a situation, emotional enlightenment and the overview you might need to organise your life (or a specific situation) more effectively.

Diary writing tends to be about tracking thoughts, ideas etc by date, allowing you to notice progression and notice when change occurs in a particular field, while at the same time providing you with a visual tool for keeping on top of a particular situation.

Journaling generally refers to a more spontaneous outpouring of thoughts, ideas, and emotions, which are not defined by date. Recording thoughts and feelings on paper allows you to see them objectively and change them if you want to, but airing feelings just for the sake of it is also cathartic, and leads to deeper self-knowing.

[12] **Keeping a diary makes you happier**
(https://www.theguardian.com/science/2009/feb/15/psychology-usa)

Some suggestions for diary keeping

- Eating or drinking habits
- Your health treatment record
- Job applications
- Spending
- Your experiences of something regular and specific in your life, (in order to track your changing relationship, thoughts and feelings about this thing)
- Time spent on a particular thing (either because you want to do more – piano practice for example – or because you are worried you are doing too much – watching TV for example.)

The beauty of diary keeping is the clarity you get from doing it, plus the insights to be gained into your behaviour.

Some suggestions for journaling

- Creative ideas (stories, characters, jokes, song lyrics, lines of poetry, etc)
- Emotional outpourings
- Your feelings about a person, situation or event
- Lists – gratitude lists, bucket lists, hope-for lists...

The beauty of journaling is the creative flexibility you allow yourself. There are no rules. There is no wrong way to write. There is nothing off limits.

Exercise 20 ~ Splurge Journal!

"Fill your paper with the breathings of your heart."
William Wordsworth

~

Writing down feelings and thoughts can give you a wonderful insight into yourself, your moods, your inspirations, and the way you think and feel about things. Their private nature means that you don't need to feel inhibited about what you write, which allows your thoughts a chance to breathe and feelings to emerge that otherwise might not have seen the light of day.

Over time, this exercise is a great way to develop your intuition.

- Write for 10 minutes or longer, whatever comes into your head.
- Splurge it all out and never let the pen leave the page.
- Write, write, write!
- Sooner or later you will find that your pen is leading you; that your intuition is driving you.

This exercise is especially beneficial to those of us who have been in the habit of blocking thoughts and feelings. Doing it on a regular basis will encourage thoughts to flow freely and discover what's lurking beneath consciousness!

Exercise 21 ~ Reflection Journal

"Pull out from the depths those thoughts that you do not understand, and spread them out in the sunlight and know the meaning of them."

E. M. Forster

~

Sometimes we just need to find space to think clearly about something and separate different strands of thought. When you give yourself permission to be disorganised with your thoughts and write them down without pressure, you will gradually start to see order and priorities, rather than a knotty mess of confusion. This exercise is an opportunity to reflect on your thoughts, as opposed to your emotions.

- Simply sit down with pen and paper and write down your **thoughts** about whatever it is that perplexes you – your day, your work, your relationships and so on. In doing this you release the need to hold on to everything and are easier able to disassociate them from your **emotions**.

This is a little more focused style of writing than the previous exercise, and you may find yourself asking many questions which don't have immediate answers. That's okay; the answers will come later, but with everything now on paper, you have a chance to see these thoughts objectively, and deal with them as and when you can.

Exercise 22 ~ Dream Diary

"Dreams are the royal road to the unconscious activities of the mind."

Sigmund Freud

~

Dreams reveal hidden thoughts, emotions, fears and anxieties by turning them into monsters, difficult situations, impenetrable walls or a never ending labyrinth. By creating metaphors for the unconscious mind to work with we allow it to work things through without actually having to consciously puzzle something out. But listening to those dreams, looking for repeating patterns and getting creative with them, can provide greater self-understanding and relief from anxiety.

Keep a dream diary

- Every morning upon waking, record any whole or part dreams you can remember.
- When you have been doing this for a while, look for repeating patterns or images, or people, and think about what these might represent in your life, or be trying to tell you. Free writing may help to loosen up some of your thoughts on this.
- If you have an especially interesting or vivid dream use it as a starting point for your creative writing and see what unfolds. Do the same with an upsetting dream but make sure you create yourself a happier, more satisfying ending.

5: BELIEF MATTERS

~

"Our minds influence the key activity of the brain, which then influences everything; perception, cognition, thoughts and feelings, personal relationships; they're all a projection of you."

Deepak Chopra

~

People – you, me, him next door, the rich, the poor, the sick, the strong, and everyone in between – we all have many beliefs about ourselves. We have a mixture of positive and negative beliefs; many of which are not evident but still manage to exercise a great deal of control over us.

I'm going to use the iceberg simile again here. Your mind is like an iceberg sitting in the Arctic. Your conscious mind is the bit sticking out above the water level. Your unconscious mind is the bit you can't see; the enormous wealth of thoughts underneath the water line. Just as the tip of the iceberg needs the rest of the iceberg to support it, your conscious thoughts (the ones you know about) are supported by your unconscious thoughts (the other ones underneath) – your beliefs.

The majority of these beliefs were formed in your infancy and childhood. They will have been created out of a need for safety, social approval, compliance, and many other reasons. At the time, they will have served you well, and your ego defence mechanism will want to hang on to those beliefs for all it's worth.

That does not mean your ego is right, or that those beliefs serve you well now. Let me give one example. You are a crying baby whose parent, for whatever reason, cannot comfort you. Over time, you stop crying. Your parent is pleased, relieved even, and you are rewarded in some way. There are dozens of ways this scenario might play out, and dozens of beliefs you might take away from this. One belief might be – nobody comforts me. Or, people are happy when I don't ask for help. Of course, this is hugely simplified, but it is one example.

At best, beliefs simplify our lives; they provide a shortcut to thinking through the ins and outs of every situation. At worst, beliefs, these shortcuts to thinking, act as brakes on our development and our chances of a happy fulfilled life; in other words, they limit us.

Negative self-talk, self-doubt, insecurity, poor self-image and feelings of worthlessness are a result of a belief system which does not serve you well. Repressed negative emotion (for example fear, anger, depression, jealousy, apathy, grief and pride) will all find its way to the surface somehow or other and may well manifest in unwanted behaviours – over-eating, alcohol or drug abuse, extreme anger, violent outbursts, phobias, obsessions for example – which impact on your life, and the lives of others. That's why it is important to deal with these controlling beliefs. (*[13])

---

[13] For a deeper understanding about beliefs and how they affect you, take a look at **Who's the Boss of You** | Kris Williams | Krisalys Books 2015

There are three kinds of beliefs which get in our way: flawed beliefs, illogical beliefs, and self-limiting beliefs. Many beliefs cross over the boundaries and fall into more than one category. It could be argued that all beliefs are self-limiting.

Flawed beliefs are often left over from childhood. For example, 'I don't like vegetables.' But have you tried vegetable lately? Have you tried ALL of them? Cooked in every possible way? Just because something was true once, does not mean that it is always true. Plenty of vegetable devouring adults didn't like vegetables when they were children. But they changed. Why should you be any different?

Illogical beliefs don't actually add up when you put them under scrutiny. For example, 'I once got food poisoning after eating at a friend's house. My friend kept cats. Cats cause food poisoning.' Really? It's quite possible that this person has developed an illogical and invalid belief about cats to mask some other experience or memory.

Self-limiting beliefs stop you achieving your full potential and are arguably the most powerful of the hidden beliefs since they reinforce early negative thinking without ever being questioned. Beliefs like, "I'm not good enough ... pretty enough ... strong enough ... rich enough ... clever enough … etc" were probably formed at a very young age. By allowing them to influence your unconscious thought processes now you are doing yourself an injustice. These hidden beliefs need to be out in the open and changed.

If you want to change your life for the better but feel like whatever your efforts, you always end up in the same place, it is likely that your 'belief baggage' is a bit too heavy and needs a clear out.

Getting clear is not about going over old problems for the sake of it. That would be of no value and all you would end up doing is making yourself less clear. If you focus on a problem you will only be reminded of the problem. Getting clear is about understanding a situation, emotion or thought and giving yourself the option to let it go. For most people, not being clear is the biggest obstacle to happiness.

You may find that solutions come to you when you let go of things, or you may just feel lighter and more able to be happy in the present.

The exercises which follow will help you uncover what you believe. They will help you think about ways to change the limiting beliefs and install new beliefs for your subconscious mind to work from.

A word about trauma

It's possible that some of your beliefs are a result of traumatic experience, in which case you are unlikely to want to relive those memories in order to expose the beliefs they have instilled in you. It's fair to say that writing specifically about traumatic events or memories, particularly if these have been locked away for any period of time, will be at best difficult and at worst painful.

There is evidence to suggest that writing about trauma can impact on health and emotional well-being for up to 6 months. (*14) However, if you are feeling up to it and have the stamina to persevere, after this period both the physical and emotional health improves. So, whilst writing about trauma may not feel especially beneficial at the time, there are clearly long-term benefits.

Pick and choose the exercises which follow and do only what you feel ready to do.

---

[14] **Confronting a traumatic event: Toward an understanding of inhibition and disease** | James W Pennebaker & Sandra K Beall | Journal of Abnormal Psychology, Aug 1986 (http://dx.doi.org/10.1037/0021-843X.95.3.274)

Exercise 23 ~ Notice What You Say

"Who looks outside, dreams. Who looks inside, awakes."

Carl Jung

~

This is a listening exercise as much as a writing exercise and requires some self-awareness. If you already keep a journal of your thoughts or feelings, you may find it an appropriate starting point to uncover your underlying beliefs; if you don't keep a journal, follow this exercise from the beginnings and return to it time and again for further illumination.

- Pay attention to the things you say and the conversations you have.

- Keep a notebook handy and jot down the main themes of your conversations, as and when you notice them. This will get easier over time.

- After a few weeks look back at your notebook and see if you can spot a pattern. Do you find yourself repeating the same kind of thing? Do your interactions with others tend to have some kind of theme? For example, lack of money, time, or love. The pattern relates to a belief that you have.

- Write down what you think the belief is. If it's a limiting belief, you can do one of the later exercises to tackle and eradicate it. If it's a positive, beneficial belief, then leave it right there where you've got easy access to it!

Exercise 24 ~ Back to Your Roots

"It is wisdom to know others; it is enlightenment to know one's self."

Lao-Tzu

~

Most of your beliefs were formed during your childhood. We're not blaming parents or carers who probably did the best they knew how at the time, but we are trying to get to the roots of some of your core beliefs.

Try to remember what your parents, carers, and adult influences said about any of the topics below. (Remember, they were acting and speaking as a result of their own belief systems, which may, in turn, have been formed during their own childhoods, and so on.) Dig deep, and remember their opinions because most likely these are also things which influence your hidden belief system now.

Money	Sex
Relationships	Education
Body image	People
Self Expression	Selfishness
Rejection	Failure/Success
Mistakes	Valuing yourself
Religion	Anger

Feel free to add anything else to this list if it feels relevant.

It's quite possible you've never thought about some of these subjects before, in which case this alone should give you a deeper insight into the contributing factors to what makes you who you are.

Follow On

- Pick one word from the above list – something which resonates with you particularly.
- You know what your adult influences said about it, but what does it mean to you?
- Write a list of about 10 words which you associate with it now.
- Compare the two pieces of writing. Are they different/the same? Can you see a connection between what you learned as a child and what you believe now? Was it what you expected?

This exercise is about providing illumination, and will give you something to work with later. You can go through each topic in turn and uncover more about your beliefs if you so wish.

Exercise 25 – How Beliefs Affect You

"Believe you know all the answers, and you know all the answers. Believe you're a master, and you are."

Richard Bach

~

If you've completed the previous two exercises, you may have a better idea about how your beliefs were formed. But how do they affect you now?

This is an exercise you may return to now and again to see what's new.

- Make 4 lists of your beliefs, under the headings: My Body, My Intelligence, My Personality, and My Relationships.
- Put a tick next to everything you believe to be true. (Just because you believe something, doesn't mean it is true.)
- Pick one statement you have ticked, and write down all the reasons why this might be interpreted as a flawed, illogical or limiting belief you have about yourself.
- How does this belief make you feel?
- Do a piece of creative writing about how different your life might be if you didn't have that belief. Write yourself a picture of your life if that belief wasn't there, just to get a real feel for how it is holding you back.

By now, you should have had a glimpse what it feels like to be free of just one limiting belief. You can repeat this exercise for other beliefs, and the more you do it, the more you will feel a shift in your understanding; allowing yourself to be flexible in your beliefs about yourself, will allow you to feel happier.

Exercise 26 ~ Being Explicit and Implicit

"To find out your real opinion of someone, judge the impression you have when you first see a letter from them."

Arthur Schopenhauer

~

Some of your hidden beliefs will be found by 'reading between the lines' of what you are saying. This exercise looks at how you use explicit and implicit statements and the effect which both have.

There is no right or wrong time to use explicit or implicit statements, but it's important to be aware of the differences; being aware gives you a choice about how to use language in the future and the impression you want to make.

Explicit writing uses short direct statements to state a fact. It is a strong and obvious voice that the reader will read as authoritative. For example, 'I am determined to achieve this promotion.'

Implicit writing gets the information over in a concealed or ambiguous manner; it is what you imply with your words rather than what you say directly. For example, 'I wouldn't turn down a promotion.'

While explicit statements are direct and powerful, they can be limiting because they are definitive by nature. Implicit statements are a combination of, or entirely made up of negative words. In the above statement, although promotion is positive, the words *wouldn't* and *turn down* are loaded with negativity and raise all sorts of questions.

Both styles have their uses, but if you want to create a certain impression, it is as well to be aware of how you are creating it.

- Write a letter or a diary entry about something that has happened to you recently. Pick out the implicit or explicit statements.
- Rewrite this letter or diary entry, replacing all the implicit statements with explicit statements.
- Rewrite it again, doing the opposite.

You will now have one letter or diary entry full of explicit statements and one full of implicit statements.

- Compare the two and try to get a feel for differences.

Exercise 27 ~ Personify Your Belief

"There is nothing that can help you understand your beliefs more than trying to explain them to an inquisitor."

Frank Howard Clark

~

This is a fun and effective exercise to help you distance yourself from a negative belief you hold, and think about it in a different way.

- Pick out one of your beliefs that you would like to change.
- Imagine this belief is another person. Think about him or her and write a description of what this person looks like as if you are describing them to someone who has never seen him/her before. You can be as creative as you like!
- Describe his/her personality.
- Give him/her a name.
- Now think of all the ways that this person has impacted on your life, including all the negative consequences of this, and write a letter to this person. Tell him/her how he/she has made you feel, and how that has influenced your actions and behaviour. Tell him/her the lessons he/she has taught you. Be grateful for the deeper understanding he/she has given you. Be as open and honest with him/her as you can.

- You might also want to explain why it is time to let him/her go, and how you want to move on into the future.
- When you have finished, imagine he/she is standing before you and read them the letter out loud.

How do you feel now? Hopefully, you should be a little clearer about this belief and feel able to leave it behind.

Essential follow on

- Pick out a positive belief you have about yourself.
- Repeat the steps for this positive belief, leaving out the letting go part of the exercise. Really get a sense of why this is a good thing for you.

Doing this will reinforce all the good feelings associated with this belief and will very likely put a smile on your face for the rest of the day!

Exercise 28 ~ Challenge Your Belief

"There was a time when just about everyone believed – indeed, knew for an obvious fact – that the world is flat and the sun went around it every day. Guess what? That didn't make them right."

Adrian Savage

~

This is a similar exercise to the previous one, in that you are asked to personify your belief, but there is more of a dialogue involved.

- Follow steps 1 – 4 in Exercise 27.
- Now have a conversation with this belief. Write it out as a piece of dialogue, along the lines of a 'he said/she said' conversation.
- Ask your belief to explain his/her reasons for this belief. It's important to challenge this belief, and equally important for this belief to defend itself.
- If at the end of the dialogue, your belief has not managed to convince you that he/she deserves a place in your life, you may tell your belief that it's time to let him/her go.

By bringing hidden beliefs to the fore, you are sending a powerful signal to the unconscious mind that you are now ready to address them. Whether or not you choose to eliminate them at this point is not nearly as important as getting to know them. You certainly can't let go of something you don't know you are holding.

Exercise 29 ~ Objectifying a Belief

"Listen to your inner voice... for it is a deep and powerful source of wisdom, beauty and truth, ever flowing through you..."

Caroline Joy Adams

~

So, you've tried personifying a belief; now have a go at objectifying one. In this exercise, you're letting the belief do all the talking.

- Write down a belief you are unhappy about in your life.
- Imagine it is an object. Any object.
- Write a description of that object and represent that object in any way you can. What shape, colour and feel does it have? How does it make you feel? Get in touch with it as if you could see it in front of you, or hold it in your hands, or maybe you can hear it.
- Now ask the object if it has something to tell you and imagine that you hear an answer. Write down this answer; it will be from inside your head, but go with it. Just free flow with the writing.
- When you have finished writing, you will be clearer about that belief and the effect it has on you.

Exercise 30 ~ Installing new beliefs

"If we can once believe that success is possible, success becomes possible."

Frank Chapman Sharp

~

When you let go of a belief, it's a good idea to fill up that empty space with a new one. It is possible to let go of an unhelpful belief with relative ease, but sometimes it requires a little more effort to make sure your new belief is fully installed and working. Your biggest obstacle is self-doubt. Your critical inner voice – the one who's been shouting at you for years – will be screaming, 'this will never work'. But by feeding your conscious mind a diet of new, more empowering beliefs, it will.

They say it takes 30 days to create a habit; that is the minimum amount of time you need to spend on this exercise. If your super ego is very strong and those critical inner voices persist in trying to convince you that your new beliefs are unfounded, you may find this is something you need to return to again and again. But remember, people do change, people do control what they think and feel, and people do manage to turn their lives around for the better. Also, some things are easier to let go of than others, so do be kind to yourself along the journey.

Clearly, the more tangible your outcome, the stronger the evidence is to support your new belief. But to help any belief take roots, it will help if you collect evidence of it working in your life. You can do this by making a plan, keeping a journal and/or by using the power of creative writing.

Your new beliefs are the foundation stones for your future; these exercises will help you build on these and develop a strong sense of a better you.

- **Making a plan** involves isolating your new belief and writing down some ways you might want to prove it is working. If your new belief is that you are 'more successful' or 'happier,' for example, think about ways you can prove this to be true. Start small; record something you know you are successful at, or happy about. It doesn't matter what it is.

- Every single time you notice your own success or happiness about something, log it in a **journal** and repeat the process several times, making sure to take the time to feel the positive emotions associated with your new belief. (Proud, satisfied, amused, happy, etc).

- Repeat the steps above until you notice a shift in your thinking and feeling.

Beliefs change through evidence and through the constant reinforcing of that evidence. That's why it's good to keep a journal, to remind yourself that you can, you are, you will.

Follow on (the creative bit)

- Have a go at writing the story of how you conquered that belief.
- Project yourself into the future – a year, ten years, fifty years (you choose) – and write about your life as if that belief has been active within you throughout the intervening time.
- What are the consequences of your new belief?
- How does your life look in the future?

6: PROBLEM SOLVING

~

"If we can really understand the problem, the answer will come out of it, because the answer is not separate from the problem."

Jiddu Krishnamurti

~

Writing things down gives us a way to work through problems and uncover solutions in many areas of life. (*15)

The act of writing is essentially a dialogue with yourself. Turning thoughts and emotions to words and committing them to paper is the start of that dialogue. As soon as words are out of your head and in front of you on paper, you have the chance to see them objectively, consider their effectiveness and value, and offer different points of view. It's not the end of the conversation, but it is part of the process of understanding and deeper self-knowing.

---

[15] In her paper, **Writing and Problem Solving,** Carol Berkenkotter of Michigan Technological University, looks at how students of maths, physics, chess playing, and composition solve problems through writing. | From - Language Connections, Writing and Reading Across the Curriculum | Edited by Toby Fulwiler, Art Young, and Heidi Scott
(http://wac.colostate.edu/books/language_connections/chapter3.pdf)

Exercise 31 ~ Blood Letting!

"The best way out is always through."

Robert Frost

~

It has always been my experience that writing things down in moments of crisis acts as a pressure valve. It's not about thinking, or trying to reason with yourself; it's about screaming onto the page, bleeding out poisonous thoughts, and letting go.

All you need to do is:

- Simply sit down with a pen and paper and write. Don't stop until you have nothing else to say.
- When you are all written out, take a step back, have a cup of tea, or a bath, or a walk; just something to give you a little bit of distance from your raw emotions.
- When you come back to your paper, ask yourself if there is really any need to hang on to it. Consider destroying it – ripping, cutting, or even burning it – to signal to the unconscious mind that this 'problem' is now done with; you can let it go.
- If you are not ready to let go, repeat the process, writing out more difficult feelings with each draft until there is really nothing left to say.

As a result of doing this, you may find yourself feeling empty and numb. This is understandable; you have just created a big space inside of you where all those horrid old feelings once dwelt. I suggest you follow on from this exercise with one from the first section of this book – **Being Happy** – and fill yourself up again with positivity and good thoughts.

Exercise 32 ~ The Negative Questions

"In every moment of our existence, we are in that field of all possibilities where we have access to an infinity of choices."

Deepak Chopra

~

When you listen to self-talk, you may hear limiting questions such as, 'Why do bad things always happen to me? Why am I such a terrible person? Will I never get it right?' These sort of questions limit possibility because they only ask for answers which reinforce a negative state of mind.

Arguably a better way to ask these questions would be, 'When are good things going to happen to me? What's wonderful about me? How do I get it right?' These questions lead you round the edges of resistance and instantly get you into a better feeling place.

This is a quick fix easy exercise, but you won't do it in one sitting; it's something you will return to time and again, so keep a notebook or piece of paper handy and add to your list of questions as and when you become aware of them.

Here's how you do it:
- Fold a page of paper in half.
- On one half, make a list of the negative questions you hear yourself dwelling on.
- And on the corresponding half, see if you can replace it with a more positively phrased question which will open the door to a new emotion, a better emotion, a better thought and a maybe even a solution.

Exercise 33 ~ When You Feel Stuck

"The world of reality has its limits; the world of imagination is boundless."

Jean-Jacques Rousseau

~

When you feel stuck, you may find that a list will open your mind to the choices you have. A list of all the possible outcomes can take your mind to the thoughts and ideas you didn't know existed ... and help you become unstuck.

So, what are you stuck about? A relationship, job, what to have for dinner?

- Write it down
- Next, write a list of every possible choice you have
- Then a list of every possible outcome – whether it is good or bad or right or wrong – for every possible choice
- Write a list of every person who could help you
- Write a list of every reason why you should do what you want to do
- Write a list of every reason why you shouldn't do what you want to do
- Write a list of every alternative
- Be creative – invent your own lists

And when you have exhausted EVERY possible addition to each list, draw a line underneath and start writing again because there are always more things to add below the bottom line.

The point of this exercise is CLARITY. Laying everything out in the open provides clarity and allows you to reconsider, find solutions, or let go and move on. Chances are you will write yourself unstuck well before you have exhausted all list possibilities, but that's okay too. If you're no longer stuck, job done!

Exercise 34 ~ Your Inner Sage

"Every adversity, every failure, every heartache carries with it the seed of an equal or greater benefit."

Napoleon Hill

~

Imagine you are very old and have much wisdom to pass on. What would an older, wiser you tell the person you are now? What will you know in 20/50/70 years time?

This is an exercise which requires you to let go and trust your future self. It's a chance to project yourself into years you have yet to live and imagine your life as it will be.

- Have a conversation with yourself as if you are 111 years old.
- Write this conversation as a talking heads 'he said/she said' dialogue.
- Take it in turns to speak, and discuss your path to happiness.
- Let the older you pass on all the wisdom he or she has gathered over his or her lifetime.

The seeds of the older you are there now, lying dormant in your present; so here is your chance to let them out and borrow a little of that maturity and insight in advance.

As incredible as it may seem, this exercise is not only illuminating, it is also very effective.

Exercise 35 ~ A Story of Conflict

"You cannot solve a problem from the same consciousness that created it. You must learn to see the world anew."

Albert Einstein

~

Conflict comes in all shapes and sizes. It may be internal (wrestling with guilt, feelings of inadequacy, an important choice to make, for example) or it may be the result of something external (ill health, another person, the forces of nature, for example). Locking horns with your inner demon or battling some outside pest can be a stepping stone to something new, but if you're not up for the fight or don't know how to move on, then conflict becomes a problem and a source of tension.

If you were to write the story of a conflict – as in, the fictional story – you would start by asking these simple questions.

- Who is your character?
- What do they want?
- Who or what stands in their way?

You would then set about developing your story, attempting to solve your character's problem by providing him or her with creative solutions.

He/she may well meet more obstacles to overcome before they finally solve their problem, but in a good story, the conflict will be resolved. In most stories, there will also be a positive outcome.

In real life, the process is not so different except that, of course, a positive outcome is always required.

Writing down the answers to the following questions might help you think a little more clearly about your own conflicting situation. Alternatively, they may provide you with the basis for a story which your unconscious mind might use as a template or metaphor, for your own situation.

- Who is your character? (You, or a fictional character or your own creation.)
- What do they want?
- Who or what stands in their way?
- Why?
- How? Identify the conflict. What is the nature of that conflict?
- How does this conflict affect your character? What aspect of this conflict do they focus on most?
- Make a list of possible reasons why this particular aspect is a problem?
- What is your character going to do about it? In fiction, as in real life, this may involve seeking outside help, but your character must be the one who seeks help and he/she must be emotionally and mentally engaged in the process. In real life, this is about you having the power to make yourself happy. If your conflict is with another person and you expect them to solve the problem, you are giving them your power.

Whether you chose to write about a personal situation, or about something entirely fictional, you have the basis for a complete story here. In both cases, you acknowledge a problem, and through story-telling, you solve it. If you have chosen to write about a character (other than you) in conflict, you will inevitably identify with the feelings and emotions of that character anyway.

Exercise 36 ~ Slow Down

"The bad news is time flies. The good news is you're the pilot."

Michael Altshuler

~

Do you always feel like you are in a rush? Would you like more hours in the day? Timing is one of those things which can cause stress, and good management of time can help to reduce stress.

Traditional methods of time-management involve, working out your goals, making to-do lists, and prioritising. But, knowing how to control time in a story, may also translate into real life time management skills via a little bit of subliminal programming. To do that, you need to know how to pace your writing.

Pacing allows you to control (the illusion of) speed in your story.

Fast scenes convey action and excitement, but also up the stress levels of the reader (and writer). They give the reader a sense or urgency and importance. When you read short words, sentences, paragraphs, scenes and chapters, you feel as if things are progressing quickly. Action scenes, a series of incidents in rapid succession, cliff hangers, and quick-fire dialogue also create the illusion of speed.

Slow scenes give your characters and readers a chance to relax and catch their breath; to feel the impact of your story. They take time to develop the senses, drawing on the imagination to fully engage the mind. Long words, sentences, paragraphs, scenes and chapters, prolonged dialogue, and description all allow for periods of calm and quiet.

In real life, we experience both fast and slow moments. If life was all fast paced, or slow paced, it would be intolerably stressful or deadly boring. If timing is a particular issue for you, it may be worth giving yourself a template to control time with a little bit of creative writing.

- Choose an event which regularly causes you 'time stress.'

- Take a minute to remember the last time this happened, then write about this event, in present tense, as if it is actually happening.

- When you have finished, look back over your writing. Does it convey a sense of that rushing, frantic, pace? Have you used short words, sentences, paragraphs, scenes and chapters? Do you get a sense of action and urgency? Does a lot happen in a short space of time?

- Tweak this piece of writing to give it as much pace as you can. You want to really push the feelings of urgency as far as possible.

- When you are satisfied with your writing, take a break...

... Later

- Rewrite the same incident, but slow it down. Use long words, sentences, paragraphs, prolonged dialogue, and plenty of description; be mindful of sights, sounds, smells, and how you are feeling. Enjoy moments of calm and quiet. Stretch your creative muscle and imagine what it feels like to have all the time in the world!

- Make sure that the event ends on with a positive outcome. So for example, if you have rushed to work, make sure you get there in plenty of time.

When you have finished, you should be able to look at the two pieces of writing and take away a different feeling or level of stress from each one.

This exercise does not guarantee that you will suddenly become a more organised, time-managed person, but it does give you an alternative view of your behaviour and offer a blueprint for other possibilities.

7: PERSPECTIVE

~

"Nothing's beautiful from every point of view."

Horace

~

Point of View is the point through which we view a story; in other words, the eyes of the person who is telling the story. You can write in:

- First person i.e. **I** went to the shops. **We** went to the shops.
- Second person i.e. **You** went to the shops.
- Third person i.e. **He, she, they**, or **it** went to the shops.

In life, of course, we see the world through our own eyes. We are our own point of view. We know what we know, have done what we have done, see what we see, hear what we hear ... and so on. When something is not right in our world, we experience it primarily through our own senses, and our immediate emotions and thoughts.

Sometimes we get so caught up in that moment it's hard to remember there are alternative ways of looking at something. But imagine if you could leap backwards or forwards in time, or climb into the heart and mind of another? How would that difficult, unfathomable emotion feel then?

The following exercises give you the chance to find out.

Exercise 37 ~ Walk a Mile in their Shoes

"You never really understand a person until you consider things from his point of view... Until you climb inside of his skin and walk around in it."

Harper Lee, To Kill a Mockingbird

~

Whatever your problem or situation, you are bound to feel it more acutely than someone else. Sometimes it's good to talk to a friend and hear what they have to say about a situation, but what if there's no one around right now when this thing, this awful all-encompassing problem is really getting you down? Or what if that other person is the one causing the problem?

This exercise takes you out of yourself and sees your problem from a different point of view. Chances are, you will resist seeing a problem through an adversary's eyes, but if you can detach yourself from your own feelings, even briefly, and let that other point of view in, it may be the shortest route to overcoming a difficult situation.

- Briefly write down your problem, in your own words, from your own point of view.
- Now, imagine you were someone else. If you're in conflict with someone you might want to put yourself in their shoes for a minute and write their side of the story. Or you might want to imagine you are someone else entirely – an agony aunt, a teacher, a parent, for example – someone you trust to give good advice.
- What would they tell you in this situation? How do they see things? Do your best to imagine you are that other person and write for as long as you wish from their point of view.

There are no value judgements to be made here; this is about understanding a situation from someone else's point of view and considering other possibilities.

Exercise 38 ~ Appreciate Yourself

"The mirror is a worthless invention. The only way to truly see you is in the reflection of someone else's eyes."

Voltaire

~

For those days when you are feeling down about yourself, this exercise is great for seeing things through the eyes of someone who thinks you're wonderful. You cannot go through life being totally unappreciated, because no matter whom you are and what you may think right now, at some point in your life, someone, somewhere did – and still does – know that to be true.

(Having said that, even if you still believe you have been totally and wholly unloved, you can still do this exercise.)

- Think of someone who has loved you at any time in your life and take a few minutes to see yourself through their eyes.
- If you really cannot think of anyone who has loved you, invent someone. Imagine your perfect friend, parent or lover, and for the purposes of this exercise, see yourself through their eyes. Let your imagination love you instead.
- Write a paragraph about yourself, as if you are them. Describe what they see, hear and importantly what they feel about the person who is you.
- What are the qualities they see in you?
- What do they like about you?
- What is it that makes you special for them?

Write as clear a picture as you can, concentrating on the positive things only, and allow yourself to feel thoroughly appreciated.

Refer to this piece of writing whenever you need to.

Exercise 39 ~ Perspective of Distance

"There are truths on this side of the Pyrénées, which are falsehoods on the other."

Blaise Pascal

~

Things that happened to us five, ten, or even fifty years ago inevitably feel different to us now than they did at the time. And by the same reasoning, you are bound to feel differently about things in another year, ten years, or fifty years into the future.

Changing your perspective is one way to see around the edge of a problem, and when you do, you may also find a solution.

This two-part exercise gives you the perspective of distance, even when things are on top of you in the present. The first part highlights how your feelings have already changed and how you have moved on from past events. The second part allows you to find perspective on a current event by projecting yourself into the future.

Part 1 – In past tense

- Write about something that happened in your childhood; it doesn't matter what it is. You do not have to go into too much detail; just say enough to give it some meaning and importantly, try and remember the feelings you had about it then.
- When you have finished writing, notice how your adult perspective has taken away some of the impact of the event.

Part 2 – In present tense

- Write about something which is bothering you now.
- Briefly describe the problem.
- Project yourself a month, a year or five years into the future (or more) and imagine how you will feel about it then. Write down your future thoughts and your feelings on the matter, but continue to write in present tense, as if it is happening now.

Chances are, you will feel differently, and if so, better equipped to find the perspective you need in the present.

Exercise 40 ~ The Optimist Within

"Optimism is the faith that leads to achievement; nothing can be done without hope."

Helen Keller

~

We all have moments of optimism and pessimism, but it's the optimist who lays down the gauntlet of hope. And hope is important. It's something we often forget, or it is drummed out of us at an early age when we are told, "Don't get your hopes up!" Many of us grow up scared to be hopeful or positive about the future in case we are let down.

But there are real long-term benefits associated with having a positive outlook (*16) which include:

- Increased life span of up to 20%
- Lower rates of depression
- Lower levels of distress
- Greater resistance to the common cold
- Better psychological and physical well-being
- Reduced risk of death from cardiovascular disease
- Better coping skills during hardships and times of stress

---

[16] **Positive thinking: Stop negative self-talk to reduce stress** | Mayo Clinic (*http://www.mayoclinic.com/health/positive-thinking/SR00009*)

This quick exercise will help you connect with the Optimist within you, and I've included it in this section because it offers you a perspective from an aspect of yourself that might not always be willing to show his or her face!

- Think about an upcoming situation or event which you feel negatively towards.
- Imagine for a moment that you feel optimistic about it instead. Indulge yourself here; it may feel like fantasy, but the reality is that you don't know what will happen.
- Write an account of the **best possible scenario** for this event, and really focus on the positive feelings you might experience. (You can write this in past, present or future tense.)
- Then underline all the emotion words. Did you use words like excited, thrilled, and hopeful?

Does this help you feel more positively about this event?

You don't know what will happen in the future. If you look at the problem, you will only ever see the problem. Your expectations may be bleak, but now is the only moment you have in which to change things. You can't change the past; you can't change the future, although you can influence it. You can change the present.

Being open to the possibility of things getting better is a good starting point, so take the time to look at life through an optimist's eyes.

8: GOALS

~

"The tragedy of life doesn't lie in not reaching your goal. The tragedy lies in having no goals to reach."

Benjamin Mays

~

Goals are important.

Goals get you out of bed each morning; they motivate you.

Goals, of all shapes and sizes, are your reasons to be alive.

Goals tell you you're in charge of your life.

Goals give your life purpose.

When you actively work towards your goals, as opposed to leaving them sat on the dream shelf, they may stretch you or push you out of your comfort zone, but this is how you grow.

Achieving your goals boosts your confidence, makes you more self-reliant and improves your outlook on life. If you can achieve this thing, maybe you can achieve this other, bigger, thing?

Put simply, goals help you to be all that you can be.

The exercises in this section will help you to be clear about your goals, but will also help you manage them so that you are empowered, rather than overwhelmed by your goals.

Exercise 41 ~ Contrast and Clarity

"If you don't know where you are going, you will probably end up somewhere else."

Lawrence J. Peter

~

Sometimes we get so locked into wanting something to be different, that we find ourselves focusing on what we don't want and forgetting the rest. But this doesn't have to be bad news! Acknowledging what you don't want is an important starting point in the journey of finding what you do want. This exercise is a very good way to find that clarity. It is both enlightening and helpful and can be used in a variety of different situations; giving clarity of purpose for a particular event, relationship or problem, or when thinking about the bigger life questions.

- Take a piece of paper and fold it lengthways down the middle.
- At the top of the left-hand side write CONTRAST.
- At the top of the right-hand side, write CLARITY.
- On the CONTRAST side, list all the things which are troubling you. Write down any beliefs you have about the situation. Write down anything which comes up. For example, *I am sick of being fat*.

- When you have finished, read it back to yourself and then on the right hand, CLARITY side, write what you want to happen/to feel/to think. For example "I am sick of being fat" may become, "I want to be slimmer."
- Do that for each statement, and as you clarify each one, cross out the statement on the left-hand side.

When you have finished with this list, you may want to rewrite the clarified list of your desires. Write it as a new list, a song, a poem, a letter or a statement of intent; whichever you choose is good. The aim of this exercise is to clarify your goals, and in so doing, switch your focus to the **solution** rather than the problem.

However, clarity alone will not make your dreams and desires reality.

Do the next two exercises to bring further clarity to your goals and desires.

Exercise 42 ~ What Your Goals Mean

"Your vision will become clear only when you look into your heart."

Carl Jung

~

This exercise builds on the previous one and works to develop a sense of what your goals will mean to you and how they might make you feel.

- Look at your clarified list of desires from the previous exercise. (If you have not done the previous exercise, write a list of your goals, both short and long term.) Think about personal goals, ones related to your physical health and body, educational, professional, creative, emotional and material goals. Don't leave anything out.

- Go through each goal in turn and list the feelings you expect to get from having these things. (For example, happiness, satisfaction, success, recognition, etc.) Don't pour over it for hours; your first reactions are usually the best. This second list is the essence of what you truly desire.

- Choose one thing from your list which seems to have some special resonance with you; maybe it is repeated several times or maybe you feel it is the one thing at the root of the others.

- Now for this one feeling, imagine you already feel like that and write a paragraph about how your life looks, sounds and feels once you have mastered that feeling. Write in the present tense.

This exercise is designed to help you feel positive about this desire and by writing in the present tense (as if you already have what you want) you know that it is possible for you to already feel this way. It is proof that somewhere inside you already do feel that way.

Exercise 43 ~ Small Chunk your Goals

"The journey of a thousand miles begins with one step."

Lao Tzu

~

I'm going to give you a warning; if you only ever focus on a distant goal, you might forget to appreciate the journey; plus, a large amount of time spent in a state of non-achievement may feel more like failure than success. (*17)

So this exercise is about the action you take towards your goals. It is about the journey, the landmarks along the way, and the pleasure to be gained from visiting those places on a daily basis, because doing one thing every day means achieving something every day. Alongside the continuous forward momentum which will eventually lead you to your ultimate goal, you are rewarded with a constant supply of successful 'job done' moments.

---

[17] **Want to succeed? You need systems not goals** | Oliver Burkeman | The Guardian, 2014
(http://www.theguardian.com/lifeandstyle/2014/nov/07/systems-better-than-goals-oliver-burkeman?CMP=fb_gu)

Can you see the road ahead clearly?

If the answer is YES, then divide your goal into small manageable chunks – write them down – and do one thing every day.

If the answer is NO, do the following exercise.

Think about all the possible routes to your goal.

- Write down anything that comes to you. Be free with your thoughts – these are only words; they can be changed. They are meant as ideas and starting points only.

- Make a daily TO DO list – keep it manageable – think, 'What single small thing will take me closer to my goal today?' (Running 100 metres? Swimming a mile? Writing a letter? Eating a plate of vegetables? Filling out a job application? Making a phone call? Learning ten new Spanish words? Finishing an essay? …)

- Tick off daily goals once they are achieved.

By doing this exercise you are creating a habit of achievement. Not only is this good for you psychologically, it is also taking you a little nearer your goal every day. And if you need to tweak your TO DO list occasionally and re-evaluate the process, or even adjust your final goal, that's good too. The writing process signals your commitment to getting to where you want to be.

Exercise 44 ~ Planning the Moment

"You may not control all the events that happen to you, but you can decide not to be reduced by them."

Maya Angelou

~

Whilst imagining your goals and planning for them is important, there is some research to suggest that you should also visualise and plan for the **obstacles** you might meet on the way. (*[18]) This exercise will give you a new perspective on a perceived difficult moment in the future.

- Imagine a forthcoming event in your life that you feel negatively towards.
- Jot down (separately) **everything you think could go wrong** and any problems that concern you, and put these pieces of paper in a container.
- Spend a couple of minutes picturing the scene in your head, before you arrive at the event.
- Then start writing. Describe the event as you would like it to go, ideally. For example, "I walk into the room feeling calm and in control…"
- Every few minutes, pick a random event from the container.

---

[18] **Positive fantasies about idealized futures sap energy** | Heather Barry Kappes & Gabriele Oettingen | Journal of Experimental Social Psychology 47 (2011) 719–729
(http://www.psych.nyu.edu/oettingen/Barry%20Kappes,%20H.,%20&%20Oettingen,%20G.%20(2011).%20JESP.pdf)

- Think about the best course of actions for this event and how you can realistically act and feel to turn this to your advantage.
- Warning – don't duck out of any scenario. Stay with it and find that best course of action.

Basically, this is your battle plan! If something unforeseen happens, because you have already practised turning problematic events to your advantage, it will be easier for you to meet these unexpected challenges and create a new solution to the problem when you need to.

Exercise 45 ~ Your Perfect Day

"Yesterday is but today's memory, and tomorrow is today's dream."

Khalil Gibran

~

Here's an exercise which can help you focus on what you want in life, and at the same time make use of your sensory awareness. Most people are dominant in one and sometimes two senses, but we have five senses constantly bombarding us with information about our world. When you take the time to give all these senses a mental work-out, your feeling experience is so much the richer.

- Imagine you have achieved everything you want in your life and that life could not be better. What would actually make it a perfect day for you?

- When you have an image of what life will be like, take a pen and paper and describe your perfect day, from the moment you wake up to the moment you go to sleep.

- Use your senses to describe the look, feel, smell, taste and sound of everything you experience.

- When you have finished, read it back to yourself and if anything doesn't feel as good as it can possibly be, then tweak it. Get it right.

Have a look at this perfect day picture you have created with words on a regular basis, and make sure you activate a good feeling state when you do. If something no longer rings true, then adjust your description and make it right for you in the present. It's okay to change your mind; the point is to climb inside the pleasure and the joy you will feel on that perfect day and experience it as something in the present, rather than some far away future moment.

9: CONNECTING

~

"Words are singularly the most powerful force available to humanity. We can choose to use this force constructively with words of encouragement, or destructively using words of despair. Words have energy and power with the ability to help, to heal, to hinder, to hurt, to harm, to humiliate and to humble."

Yehuda Berg

~

Although the act of writing may seem like a solitary occupation, when you write for an audience it's not. The words you write communicate information, emotion, or both, and paint pictures in the minds of your readers. Whether you are writing a story, a poem, an autobiographical account of something, or even a piece of non-fiction, you are creating a shared experience; shared between you and the reader.

From a reader's point of view, we experience your story, your pictures, your life, and invest some of our own emotional resonance in whatever you have written.

Writing is a way to connect with others.

You are, of course, at liberty to keep all of your writing private. Certainly, some pieces of writing should never be shared. But if you do feel like using this gift to communicate with another, here are a couple of exercises to get you started.

Exercise 46 ~ Write a Feeling Letter

"It takes two to write a letter."

Elizabeth Drew

~

Writing a letter to someone is a very effective way to give you clarity about the way you feel. When you write to another person, you are connecting with their energy and bringing emotions and thoughts (about them) to the surface, which you might not otherwise allow yourself to feel. Beyond that, writing a letter can help to clear a feeling (if it is not one you want), or reinforce a feeling (if it is positive and life affirming).

If you are writing to clarify, clear, or reinforce feelings about a person or a situation9:

- Say everything you want to say.

- Concentrate on getting everything out.

- Don't worry about grammar, or spelling, or the way your words are ordered. (Time for that later.)

- Express yourself and don't hold back! (No one else need ever read this.) Write how this other person or situation made/makes you feel, how it has affected your life, (for better or worse), and what choices you have made because of their actions.

- Once written, read it back to yourself.

By now, you should have a clearer idea of what it is you are really feeling and/or thinking.

If it was a negative or destructive emotion – anger, resentment, jealousy, for example – your writing should have provided a catharsis. I suggest tearing this letter into tiny pieces and destroying it forever. There is no point in hanging on to these emotional outpourings, and the physical destruction of them sends a very strong message to your unconscious mind that you have moved on.

If your feelings were more positive – gratitude, love, or admiration, for example – you should be left with a warm fuzzy feeling inside! You may want to consider sending your letter and sharing those feelings but you don't have to. The main purpose of this exercise is to acknowledge your good feelings and to be able to reignite them for a while.

If there are still things you feel unclear or unhappy about, write another letter or do another exercise.

Write a reply

If you want to extend this exchange, consider writing a reply. This is a most effective way to see something from another person's point of view and get outside of your own emotional world view.

- Imagine you are the recipient of your letter.
- What have you got to say back?

Write to yourself

You don't just have to write letters to other people; writing to yourself is also very therapeutic and will increase your self-awareness.

- **Try writing a letter to yourself in the past**; to a younger you, either at a time when you were in difficulty or when you did something you felt especially proud of. In both cases, use the wisdom you have gained since to advise and nurture your younger self.
- See what happens when a younger you replies!
- **Try writing a letter to yourself in the future**; to an older you to thank them for all they have done for you over the years, tell them of your plans for the intervening years, or give them a happy memory to warm the cockles of their heart.
- **Or, try writing to yourself in the present**. Give yourself a pep talk, or a pat on the back, and tell yourself the things you need to hear right now.

Exercise 47 ~ What Can You Give?

"There is no exercise better for the heart than reaching down and lifting people up."

John Holmes

~

In almost any article or book you read, one of the foundation stones of happiness is doing things for others. Acts of kindness are not just good for others; they're good for you, the giver. Doing things for others can improve your health, develop empathy, create stronger connections and deeper understanding, and ultimately make a happier society for everyone. Scientific evidence has shown us how kindness changes the brain, improves the heart and immune system, and may be an antidote to depression. (*19)

Here are a few ideas for how you can give back to the world with your writing.

- Write a letter to someone to tell them how they have influenced or changed your life for the better, and of course, say thank you.
- Visit a retirement home and offer to write down someone's memories.
- Write down your favourite happiness quotes and leave them somewhere for a stranger to find.

---

[19] For more about this, take a look at **Why Kindness is Good For You** | David R. Hamilton Phd | Hay House 2010

- Write a list of compliments you might pay to other people, and give them away, one by one. Receiving a compliment on paper is something the recipient can keep, and every time they refer to it, they won't be able to help but feel a glow of positivity.
- Write to a stranger; someone who is lonely, isolated or just in need of cheering up: an elderly neighbour, a prisoner on death row, (*20) or a soldier fighting overseas. (*21)
- Write about your experience of something difficult, something you were able to overcome, to inspire and give hope to others in your position.
- Write a story to read to a child, and bring a little magic into their life.
- Write a list of ten things you love about someone, put it in a little box, and give it to them to keep...

Look up the 2013 Kindness Challenge Winner - Hannah Brencher, More Love Letters – video on YouTube to see just how far you can take this. (*22)

And of course, think up your own ideas too.

---

[20] **Human Writes** is a non-profit, humanitarian organisation which befriends people on death row in the USA **. (http://www.humanwrites.org/becoming-a-penfriend.php)**
[21] **Forces Penpals** | (https://www.forcespenpals.co.uk/write-to-soldiers)
[22] **More Love Letters | 2013 Kindness Challenge Winner**, Hannah Brencher (https://www.youtube.com/watch?v=h6VgNzJ04z8)

Exercise 48 ~ Developing Empathy

"I don't like that man. I must get to know him better."

Abraham Lincoln

~

Sometimes in life, there are people who for whatever reason, we do not like or get on with. The trouble with this is that your feelings towards them will likely have no effect on them, but will serve to make you feel bad instead. Every time you think an uncomfortable or nasty thought about someone else, that thought affects your well-being, not theirs.

For your own benefit, it is better if you can think and feel differently about those people who irritate or annoy you.

Using the polarity change exercise from earlier (**Exercise 14 ~ What's in a Word**) this exercise helps you to see outside of the box; to stop yourself getting caught up in a totally negative view of someone which will, in turn, help you feel better in yourself.

- Think of someone who you do not like or get on with, and choose one of their character traits that you especially dislike.
- Write this down on paper and disassociate it from that person.
- Create a general list of words associated with this trait.
- Divide them into two lists – one negative and one positive.
- Find one word of positive polarity to replace each negative word and write a new list.
- Write a paragraph describing the other person using words from the positive list.

10: FICTIONALISING YOUR LIFE

~

"All autobiography is storytelling; all writing is autobiography."

J. M. Coetzee

~

Therapeutically, the benefit of fictionalising your life is that it helps you to see things in a different light and helps you to be objective; it helps you to see other points of view, distances you from the immediacy of your own emotions and broadens your outlook. It is metaphor, plus perspective, plus creative license; all rolled into one. You have a chance to rewrite your life and to some extent, experience the life of your dreams (and/or nightmares) by changing the past, creating the future and embellishing the present.

Metaphor provides a distance to the immediacy of the emotions but fictionalising your life goes beyond this. You are the subject of your story, while your life events provide the narrative; you are free to play with the representation of these in any way you choose. What matters in fictional biography is that tiny seed of truth your story flowers from, because within that seed is the essence of the feelings and emotions you did not allow yourself to feel first time round.

Fictional biography links the emotion to the event and in so doing, helps to facilitate a change. The exercises in this section offer you the opportunity to fictionalise your life, while at the same time creating it anew.

Exercise 49 ~ Plot Your Own Story

"You write your life story by the choices you make. You never know if they have been a mistake. Those moments of decision are so difficult."

Helen Mirren

~

Stories, unlike life, tend to have a defined structure which makes them easy to navigate. The simplest of stories will have a beginning, middle and end.

> John met Janet.
> John and Janet fell in love.
> John and Janet were married.

If your own life were as simple as that, it would be boring!

In reality, John and Janet will do all sorts of wonderful things, but they will probably argue sometimes, doubt their feelings for each other, break up and get back together again. Maybe John is ill, or Janet loses her job. Maybe their families disapprove of their choice of partner etc … It's the problems which make John and Janet's story interesting. It's the problems – which John and Janet must learn to overcome – that give their lives meaning and momentum.

And I don't just mean bad problems; maybe John and Janet are going on holiday and don't know how to book a flight. That's a problem too, and it needs a solution if they are ever going to get to sunny Spain. Good and bad, it's their problems which give them a chance to discover something new about their lives and find a resolution.

Of course, in real life, resolution of one thing is not the end of the story; one thing will always lead to another. But navigating our way through obstacles and finding solutions to problems is something we all have to do before we reach our goals. If you find yourself in a position where you feel stuck, or feel that the solution is just too far out of reach, you may find that fictionalising the situation will provide the space for clarity and objectivity to take over.

This exercise builds on **Exercise 35 ~ A Story of Conflict,** and is one I use to create a simple plot plan for my own stories, but it works for real life problems too.

The important thing is to be creative with your thinking and try to disassociate yourself from the story character, whilst keeping the real life problem as near to real events as you can. In other words, let your fictional character solve your real life problem.

So, write down …

- Who is your protagonist? I.E. The person this story is about.
- What do they want?
- Why do they want it?

NB: These three questions all relate to you. Even though you are fictionalising here, to use this exercise therapeutically you/your character needs to want the same things you do, for the same reasons.

- Who or what is against your protagonist?
- Why are they in opposition to your protagonist?
- How do they (try to) prevent your protagonist realising their goals?

NB: This is what's against fictional you; it is the obstacle to be overcome and the cause of the conflict in your life. It may be that you are your own problem – your lack of self-esteem, for example, may be holding you back from applying for that job – or the obstacle may be another person or a physical presence of some description, an illness for example. A very simple story might have only one obstacle, but the more obstacles you have, the more complex the problem and the more tension there will be.

- Think of some ways your protagonist might overcome each problem. Every time your protagonist finds a solution, you reinforce and strengthen their ability and determination to fulfil their goal.
- What is the final obstacle?

NB: This is the climax of your story. It's about as bad as it can be now for your protagonist. You may wonder how your protagonist can possibly get out of this one … but think outside the box and let your unconscious mind come up with a solution.

- How's it all going to end? Give your protagonist an end to their misery. Let them solve the problem you have been struggling so hard with, and then go away and let this sink in.

As a purely creative exercise, this is a good way to develop a story from scratch. As a therapeutic exercise, it's a great way of walking around, climbing over, or steamrollering through obstacles! The act of writing this story will not solve your problem in real life, but it will set your conscious and unconscious mind on the path to finding solutions, rather than sitting back and feeling trapped.

When you have this basic plot plan, have a go at writing the story and always write a happy ending.

Exercise 50 ~ Write Your Own Fairy Tale

"Fairy tales are more than true: not because they tell us that dragons exist, but because they tell us that dragons can be beaten."

Neil Gaiman

~

Another way to write your own story is to turn it into a fairy tale.

In 1928, the Russian critic Vladimir Propp (*23) wrote Morphology of the Folktale in which he explains his theory that fairy tales were all developed from the same basic formula. These stories have clearly defined character types and the action is specific. You know where you are at the beginning, you know that something will change, you know there are certain things to be achieved and there is always a happy ending.

So this exercise is all about creating your own fairy tale. You may choose to focus on one episode or time in your life, or to see your whole life as a fairy tale. You may choose whatever style of writing you feel happy with and make the story as real or as fantastical as you wish. You may choose to write it about something entirely metaphorical.

How you approach this is up to you, as long as you follow Propp's basic formula.

[23] **Morphology of the Folk Tale** | Vladimir Yakovlevich Propp, Soviet folklorist and scholar analysed the basic plot components of Russian folk tales to identify their simplest irreducible narrative elements, 1928
(https://en.wikipedia.org/wiki/Vladimir_Propp)

Step 1 – Choose your characters

You must be the **hero**, but you can choose who will play the other roles in your fairy tale. They do not have to be real people, they may be imaginary folk or you may decide to choose different facets of yourself. (For example, if you battle with an alcohol addiction, you may choose the local publican to be the villain, or the addictive facet of your personality to be the villain.) Give all of your characters names.

- **The Hero** is the character who seeks something. You are the hero. What do you seek?
- **The Villain** is the character who opposes or blocks the hero's quest.
- **The Dispatcher** gives the hero a message to set him on his way.
- **The Donor** provides an object which has some special (magical) quality.
- **The Helper** aids the hero.
- **The False Hero** disrupts the hero's quest by making false claims
- **The Reward** – In Prop's explanation, the reward is usually a prince or princess, but in your fairy tale this may be any desired outcome. This reward is also the object of the villain's scheming.

Write very brief character descriptions for all seven characters in your story, to help you get to know them a little better.

Step 2 – Plan the action

Propp's formula has 31 very detailed stages of action. (*24) They are divided here into five more general sections which will make your fairy tale easier to manage. You can be flexible about this but try to stick to the formula as much as possible.

- **Set Up** – Something happens to upset the natural order of the family or community. The **hero** and the **villain** enter the story.
- **Inciting Incident** – The **villain** harms somebody or something, leaving the community in a state of disorder, and the **hero** is sent by the **dispatcher** to solve the problem.
- **Rising Action** – The **hero** faces many tests and challenges on his/her journey, receiving help from the **donor**, who may provide him/her with a (possibly magical) **helper**. The **hero** finally arrives at the place where he/she must fulfil his/her quest.
- **Climax** – The **hero** and **villain** meet and join in direct combat. The hero is victorious and the **villain** defeated. The initial situation is resolved and the state of disorder is settled. The **hero** returns, though a **false hero** also makes a claim
- **Resolution** – The **hero** is recognised, the **false hero** is unmasked and the **hero** receives the reward.

Now write a fairy tale of your life. And have fun!

[24] A description of each one of Propp's 31 narrative functions can be found here. **https://en.wikipedia.org/wiki/Vladimir_Propp**

Exercise 51 ~ Write your own fable

"If you read the fables ... you will know something about the person who writes them..."

Jim Crace

~

People have been telling fables for centuries. As with fairy tales, the characters are archetypes so that the story message transcends cultural and social boundaries. But unlike fairy tales, fables are short, typically with animals as characters, and they convey a moral. In the Hare and the Tortoise, for example, the moral is *slow and steady wins the race*.

The challenge of this exercise is to create your own fable. You may choose to do so for a particular situation you are involved in, or give your moral a broader message, or purely for fun ...

Make some notes on the following:

- **A moral for your Fable** – choose something which should resonate with you.

- **The conflict** – this will drive the action of the Fable, and will be the basis for the lesson to be learned.

- **The characters** – you need them to be in keeping with the tone of your Fable. For example, in the Hare and Tortoise, you needed a fast animal and a slow animal to get your point across. You may want to consider some recognised archetypes and build your characters around those, or make up your own.

For example:

Lion	~ strong, proud, fearless
Ant	~ hard working, industrious
Donkey	~ ignorant, foolish
Fox	~ clever, tricky
Bear	~ protective, patient
Butterfly	~ graceful, fragile
Monkey	~ unpredictable, clever, mischievous
Owl	~ wise, insightful, prefers to be alone
Goat	~ independent, wilful
Dog	~ loyal, selfless, forgiving

- **The setting** – where will the story take place? When will it take place? What will the weather be like? Is it relevant to the characters you have chosen?

- **The resolution** – how will the problem resolve itself? The outcome should support the moral of the story, and be satisfying and relevant to the characters involved.

With the framework in place, all you need to do now is write your fable!

Exercise 52 ~ How Is It Going To End?

"All endings are also beginnings. We just don't know it at the time."

Mitch Albom

~

Sometimes, the best place to start a story is to think about how you want it to end; this is your chance to write your own ending. I'm not talking end of life here (although you can do that too if you want to), I'm talking about the end of a phase in your life, a particular episode, a way of thinking, or a pattern of behaviour. This is your chance to create the perfect ending for you.

There are several ways to end a story but however you choose to end it must be right. By right, I mean, right for the story. A disappointing ending can ruin a great story! It doesn't have to be happy – although if you are fictionalising an episode in your own life, it's a good idea to make it so – but it does have to have a sense of completion.

To get this sense of completion, the ending should:

- be in line with what came before
- resolve the core conflict of your story
- tie up loose ends (or at least, acknowledge them)
- show how the character(s) have moved on and established a new 'normal'
- happen as a result of the protagonist's own action

When you're planning the end of a story, you need to think about all of these things, but you also need to give some thought about how you want to feel too. Do you want your ending to be happy? Shocking? Confusing? Sad?

Make some notes on:

- how you would like to feel at the end of your story
- how the ending resolves conflict and ties up loose ends
- what you have learned and how you have grown
- where you are – the physical surroundings
- who else is with you

When you've finished making notes, write the last chapter of your story. Create the ideal resolution to this little story of your life. You don't need to worry about the rest – just focus on how it all turns out.

It may not necessarily be the end you were expecting, but make sure it's one that does not disappoint.

Exercise 53 ~ The Last Sentence

"I told you I was ill."
Spike Milligan
~

What would you like your epitaph to be? Sounds morbid, but it's actually a very good exercise to think about who you are and what others will remember you for, distilled into one sentence.

This powerful sentence is a prompt for you to take stock of your life so far, and maybe help you focus on your goals and the achievement of those goals. It's also a reminder to celebrate yourself. We've all done things we should be proud of, and in our minds these things should tower over the other moments, the episodes we'd rather not remember; your own epitaph shouldn't be about regret.

If it helps, step outside of yourself and try to imagine how others might remember you. What memories would make other people smile when they remember you? What is the essence of you?

Here are some very famous epitaphs which speak volumes in few words, defining the lives and personalities of their subject.

I am ready to meet my Maker. Whether my Maker is prepared for the great ordeal of meeting me is another matter.
~ Winston Churchill

Free at last. Free at last. Thank God Almighty I'm Free At Last.
~ Martin Luther King, Jr.

The best is yet to come.
~ Frank Sinatra

I had a lover's quarrel with the world.
~ Robert Frost

Here lies the body of Richard Hind, who was neither ingenious, sober, nor kind.
~ Richard Hind

She did it the hard way.
~ Bette Davis

The only proof he needed for the existence of god was music.
~ Kurt Vonnegut

I'm a writer, but then nobody's perfect.
~ Billy Wilder

I may be gone but Rock and Roll lives on.
~ John Belushi

There goes the neighborhood.
~ Rodney Dangerfield

So we beat on, boats against the current, borne back ceaselessly into the past.
~ F. Scott Fitzgerald (from The Great Gatsby)

Hic est Edwardvs Primus Scottorum Malleus
Translation: Here is Edward I, Hammer of the Scots
~ Edward I of England

He gave all he possessed, including his life, for the wild animals of Africa.
~ Michael Grzimek

That's All, Folks!
~ Mel Blanc

... Now, what's your last sentence?

AFTERWORD

The exercises in this book are a starting point only. You may develop or adapt them to suit your own needs, or you may use them as the basis for a discussion, or a communication with others.

Bad life experiences do not have to condemn you to a life of suffering and helplessness. Research has shown that many people "can pull strength, courage, and wisdom out of misfortune" and that adversity can not only better equip you to deal with negative events, but it can also help you appreciate the positive ones.(*25)

Your introspection, while completing the exercises, has been your attempt to make sense of, and take responsibility for your life. Hopefully, it will have left you with a deeper understanding of who you are, what makes you think and feel the way you do, and why you behave in a certain way.

The act of writing also implies some commitment to change, and many of these exercises will have given you a glimpse of what change might look like and feel like if you go all the way.

I think it's important to be aware of our hidden drivers, the little voices from the past which speak so quietly yet sound so loud in our choices. Self-knowing shouldn't be about beating yourself over

---

[25] **How a Challenging Past Can Lead to a Happier Present** | Linda Graham | Greater Good Science Centre, University of California Berkeley, 2015 (http://greatergood.berkeley.edu/article/item/how_a_challenging_past_can_lead_to_a_happier_present)

the head and living in regret; it should be about opening the doors and showing self-flagellation the way out. If that's too hard to do head-on, then let your creative mind do some of the work for you. Use metaphor, use story, use poetry, use lists; use everything at your disposal to clear out the bad and welcome in the good.

We all started out as a tiny seed. We all have the potential to grow into a vibrant flowering wonder of humanity. But seeds need nurturing, and encouragement, and food for the soul. They need light and shade; they need appreciation; they need warmth, love, and acceptance for what and who they are. It's up to you to seek out that optimum growing environment.

~

"What lies behind us and what lies before us are tiny matters compared to what lies within us."

Ralph Waldo Emerson

About the author

Wendy Storer has had many different roles over the years, including waitress, barmaid, cleaner, cook, children's nanny, and some boring office jobs working for the government. She finally found her calling as a teacher and later a therapist, working with adults and children of all ages. Throughout all this, she has always found comfort in writing.

Whilst her main occupation is now writing novels for young adults, she still teaches and has never lost her interest in the positive benefits of writing as a therapeutic tool.

Originally from Essex, she now lives with her family in Cumbria, where she spends way too much time walking her dog.

www.wendystorer.ws

Printed in Great Britain
by Amazon